# TAKE YOUR
# SALES
## TO
## THE *NEXT*
# *LEVEL*

# TAKE YOUR
# SALES
## TO THE NEXT
## LEVEL

## ADVANCED SKILLS TO BUILD
## STRONGER RELATIONSHIPS
## AND CLOSE MORE DEALS

## CHARLES D. BRENNAN, Jr.

New York   Chicago   San Francisco   Lisbon
London   Madrid   Mexico City   Milan   New Delhi
San Juan   Seoul   Singapore   Sydney   Toronto

1  2  3  4  5  6  7  8  9  0    WFR/WFR    1  9  8  7  6  5  4  3  2  1  0

ISBN:  978-0-07-174543-7
MHID:  0-07-174543-2

This publication is designed to provide accurate and authoritative information in regard to the subject matter covered. It is sold with the understanding that the publisher is not engaged in rendering legal, accounting, or other professional service. If legal advice or other expert assistance is required, the services of a competent professional person should be sought.

*—From a Declaration of Principles Jointly Adopted*
*by a Committee of the American Bar Association*
*and a Committee of Publishers and Associations*

McGraw-Hill books are available at special quantity discounts to use as premiums and sales promotions, or for use in corporate training programs. To contact a representative, please visit the Contact Us pages at www.mhprofessional.com.

This book is printed on acid-free paper.

**Library of Congress Cataloging-in-Publication Data**

Brennan, Charles D.
  Take your sales to the next level: advanced skills to build stronger relationships and close more deals / by Charles D. Brennan Jr.
      p. cm.
  Includes index.
  ISBN 978-0-07-174543-7 (alk. paper)
  1. Relationship marketing. 2. Selling. 3. Sales management. I. Title.
  HF5415.55.B74 2011
  658.85—dc22

                                                    2010025346

# Contents

# TAKE YOUR
# SALES
## TO THE NEXT
# LEVEL

# Introduction

About 35 years ago, I was introduced to the profession of selling. While I was still a senior in college in Philadelphia, I was given a small territory to sell products to the industrial marketplace in the southeastern Pennsylvania area to "break me in." I was not given a salary; I had a draw against commission. I made some sales but was somewhat unsure of what I was doing. I knew that if I was to survive in this business, I needed training.

Right out of college, I enrolled in a professional selling skills course. At the time, it was a premier selling skills seminar that was offered in the area. I wanted to know how to sell. After all, I was planning to join the family business and continue a legacy that started generations before me.

Week after week for four hours at night I attended class. I did not miss a session. I listened to instructors and was amazed that there was an entire separate language, if not a code, that provided a pathway for getting people to buy what you are selling. I was fascinated to discover that a "model" existed that was a formula on how to start a conversation with a prospective customer, present an idea, and get a commitment at the end of the call.

Almost every night I practiced my skills and crafted my presentation. I remember recording and playing back my presentation for hours on end several times a week. I was told that if I practiced and internalized the skills until they were second nature, I could succeed at selling. I took this to heart—this was information I had not learned in college.

I learned more than just how to be in front of the customer. The seminar taught me the importance of pre- and postcall planning. "Wow, a game plan," I thought. "This is like preparing for a sporting event: Understand the other team's strengths and weakness and make adjustments at halftime." This was exciting to me; I was a player and a coach at the same time.

I was young and eager and scored well on many of the role-play scenarios I was assigned to complete. I graduated from the course and was anxious to apply my newly learned skills in the real world.

## Reality Check

Some of you reading this may have had the same experience I did. Armed with what I thought was a new set of skills, I went out to sell, to get new customers, and to generate more business from existing relationships. Then something happened to me that was unexpected. At times, I could not get in to see some prospective customers. Sometimes I would have to wait for a half-hour or longer to see customers, only to hear that they were not really interested in what I had to offer or that they would take my information and put it on file. Even when I called on some of the companies that we were doing business with, I was told that they already had learned everything about what I was selling from other salespeople. The client did not need anything at the moment but would call me when the opportunity arose or the need presented itself for what I was selling.

Undaunted, I carried on. I made so many calls that eventually I was able to close some new business and generate some orders from existing customers. My energy level was high, not to mention my ego. I wanted to make as many calls as possible, beat my competition, and show the family how well I could sell. At first I thought that the prospective customers that I was calling on were sincere: They would get back to me, and my timing was just not right. Some customers would grant me access and listen to my story, but nothing would happen. I was somewhat successful, but not at the level I expected.

I thought I was selling a great product and solution that would solve the customers' problems and fulfill their needs. I believed in what I was selling.

Chances are that initially you had the same drive. You felt passionate about your product or service and wanted to spread the word about its capabilities. You were a zealot and wanted to share all the great information you learned during your initial training and orientation at your company.

As I look back, that was probably one of my greatest strengths. I was persistent with an absolute belief that I had the best product available. I would actually get upset when I lost an order. How could they go in another direction? I knew what they wanted, had a good price, provided great service, yet I did not get the sale. Over the course of many years, I slowly became frustrated. Fortunately, I never got complacent. I just did not understand what was happening, why I could not get more time, interest, and business from the people I was seeing during my sales calls.

At the same time, I was approached by the school that taught me how to sell. I received an invitation to join the staff and assist in the evaluation of the role-play portion of the training prior to the students' graduation. Initially I was not enthusiastic about this opportunity. But after several discussions with my father, he suggested it might be a way for me to listen to the instructors again to pick up any additional pointers and insight that would help me with some of my stalled relationships. He said that it would be a way to keep me sharp. So, with some hesitation, I agreed. Little did I know that this decision would actually form the foundation of my career path.

## Gut Check

Night after night, I listened, commented, and graded the students based on the information that was taught to me when I went through the class several years before. I did this for about a year, until one evening it hit me like a ton of bricks. I finally understood what was going on in my sales world. For the last 12 months or so, I had listened to some great and not-so-great presentations. I probably heard several hundred sales presentations. Then one night I listened to a presentation from a student who was in my industry. After I listened to his "great presentation," I realized that what he was saying was just like my presentation and probably like everyone else in my industry's "great presentation." At that moment I also felt humbled in the understanding that my presentation probably wasn't that much better than someone else's mediocre presentation. From the customer's point of view, they were all the same.

This was unexpected. I was disappointed. I thought I had reached a level of proficiency, and I now realized that I wasn't even scratching the surface. I now understood that many of my prospective customers were actually being polite to me. They were granting me access, their time and interest, and I failed them by boring them with the same old story that almost everyone else was providing. In retrospect, I guess I was lucky to be getting the business that was given to me. I am surprised that some of my customers did not fall asleep on me! It was a revelation: cookie-cutter presentation and minimum amount of questions and involvement.

It was quite a turn of events, from believing I was doing well to the realization that maybe I was just run of the mill. I tell this story at the start of many of my live training sessions. I am guessing that a number of you reading this can relate to this. If we think about it, the customers whom we call on probably see five or more salespeople each day. Let's do the math for a quick minute. That is twenty-five meetings per week, about one hundred for the month and over a thousand for the year. You want to bet there are a lot of boring meetings in those numbers?

The concepts and content you are about to receive from this book will tell you how to move some of your customers to the next level.

The book is about moving a select few of your customers to purchase more from you. In the business world, moving only a select few forward is what makes the difference in a mediocre year versus getting the award at the national meeting. Let's read on and see if we can get you the award!

# Why Business Relationships Stall Out and Reach a Peak

## A Client's Perspective

A friend and neighbor of mine is a portfolio manager for a very large mutual fund. He is contacted regularly by salespeople from brokerage firms seeking to relay investment ideas generated by the analysts in their firms. On most days, he receives at least 500 e-mails. He deletes 300 of them after a 5-second glance, and about 100 more after a 10-second scan. He typically will not take a live call from a salesperson, even though he will receive up to 100 voice mails per day. He routes them to his voice mail to control the pace at which he listens. During a normal week, up to 100 different firms will call.

My friend shared with me that he spends several hours each day sifting through the noise, trying to find the occasional nugget of useful information or actionable idea. The overwhelming majority of calls and e-mails he receives provides no incremental value from the salespeople. They are merely passing along, verbatim, a research note produced by one of their analysts.

## Facing Facts

Let's face it; we are doing the same thing everyone else in our space is doing. We ask our questions, present our solutions, and try to gain commitment. Every day, we make our calls, report back to our managers, and listen to our directives. Every once in a while we are asked to attend a couple of sales skills or product training programs. But, by the end of the day, did we learn something new to make headway? To make matters worse, our goals get increased and our time can be manipulated with activities that are non-sales-related. For example, another course on compliance is not going to help me get more business.

Chances are that most people reading this book know how to sell. I would assume that you probably have a handful of relationships with people whom you would consider advocates, meaning that the individual customer or company is buying pretty much everything possible from you. You have great relationships. You partner with them, and they see tremendous value in what you offer. Because of these relationships, you have validated your abilities and have demonstrated the skills you need to advance a relationship to the highest level—an advocate or loyalist for your product or service.

You may have a couple of, or even many, great relationships, but there is a good possibility that you also have a greater number of relationships that are not where you want them to be. For whatever reason, over a period of time (which seems to be about a year), relationships reach a plateau and stall out. Prospective or existing customers know what you have to offer but are unwilling to move their relationship forward with you. This book is about moving those relationships forward and keeping your advocates from the competition. After all, your top customer is the competition's number one target.

# Breaking Down the Marketplace

Let's break down the marketplace and determine what contributes to your success. Those of you reading this book for the most part either sell a product or some type of service. Knowing that, I would like to focus not on what you are selling, but on how you are going about it (for right now). Eliminating for the moment your product or service, let's take a look at how you go to market.

## Customer Categories

To move relationships forward, you need to determine the type of customers you are calling on and how their viewpoint affects what they do or do not do in the marketplace. Allow me to introduce three customer categories. They are: frequent, moderate, and occasional.

The *frequent* customer is the customer who is involved in the ongoing repetitive purchase of a product or service. This customer could be someone like a physician, who will prescribe the same drug for many patients year in and year out. This customer could also be someone like a purchasing agent at a company. This person gets involved in the purchase of consumable or disposable items like paper products, supplies, parts, or repetitive services. The frequent customer category might be considered the most difficult category. This customer is familiar with your product or service and has made a determination to move forward with your product or service or not. Use for your services could be extensive. Customers such as these like to move on once a decision has been made. Access is decent if they are purchasing your product and appreciate the attention. However, if you are not the selected vendor, access can be limited. These customers are extremely busy and do not see a need to reevaluate their decision at the present time. This is the classic category to which the topics in our upcoming chapters should be applied.

The next category of customer is the *occasional* customer. This customer deals with products or services that are purchased once every several years. This type of sale tends to involve a larger capital expenditure, such as for raw materials, computers, phone systems, an ultrasound machine for a hospital, the selection of a firm to provide a service (law or accounting), or customized software for a company. The occasional customer is the person who is less likely to reach a plateau in the relationship. For the most part, the selection committee may have limited knowledge of your product or service and is willing to hear your story. These customers are tasked with an initiative to purchase a product or service that will have significant impact on the company, a department, or the way the company does business. Throughout the decision-making process, access is normally good and a number of individuals will be involved in the selection process. The issue of an incumbent vendor may not exist; however, on occasion there could be a prior relationship that complicates things in this category. The issue is whether customers have a past relationship with a provider of the product or service they are looking to purchase. For example, a company may say, "We are an IBM shop," meaning that most of the equipment it has purchased in the past for other departments or facilities has been the IBM brand. If this is the case and you are not selling IBM products, the road to closing the sale may be a bit more challenging. Getting the customer to listen to what makes you different and demonstrate the willingness to "break ranks" will take more effort from you.

The last category, the *moderate* customer, fits in between the two categories just mentioned. This customer can possibly purchase your product or service several times a year. This category would include customers providing services like investments, banking, and insurance. Moderate customers may be familiar with you, your company, and what you are selling, but they will make decisions and purchases only for what you sell a few times a year. This category has potential for increased business if they are approached more frequently or in a better or more appropriate way or differently to generate more interest. Once these customers make a decision, unless the selected provider makes a mistake or lacks follow-up and due diligence, their expectations are met. This customer category will not be proactive in reaching out to buy more, even though the moderate customer could have the most potential to buy more from you. This is the category where the most impact can be made. Improved communication with customers in this category can increase sales.

Determining which of the three categories of customers—frequent, moderate, and occasional—your customer falls into is key to your approach and determining the customer's perception of you and your offerings.

One of the first steps in moving business relationships forward and determining why they stall is to find out what category your customer is in. Once you determine the category, you gain more insight as to why things are happening, either in your favor or not.

## Getting through the Day

Let's take a look at your y customer. Chances are your customer is busy. Busy customers are probably nice people (lets hope!) but they can be stressed out. What you have to realize is how they go about their day. Allow me to explain. Several years ago, I read an interesting book called *How Doctors Think*, written by a physician by the name of Jerome Groopman. The book was recommended to me because I was frustrated with the care my father was receiving. I derived a number of insightful pieces of information from the book, which I refer to throughout this book.

In reference to the customer category, Dr. Groopman makes an interesting point about how doctors go through their day. Dr. Groopman discovered that there were two ways physicians would approach their day, responsibilities, and activities. One way is that they truly care about what they are doing and are willing to spend time to consult with their patients.

These doctors probably got involved with medicine because they wanted to make a difference and do not worry when their schedule is running late. These physicians will spend the appropriate amount of time with patients, even if all they can do is consult and point the patient in the right direction. The other type of doctor just wants to get through their day. There are a certain number of patients to see and time allotted to see them. These doctors will stay on track and not allow idle time to be spent with the patient. This is the type of person who will only do what is required, and nothing else. The clock is this person's friend and enemy. For a salesperson, this type of person is difficult to spend time with and views change as troublesome, because change takes time and effort, something they don't want to do.

## Customer Subsets

I believe that you can further categorize the three customer categories—frequent, moderate, and occasional—into two subsets. Is your customer the type who is willing to learn and improve upon what he or she is doing? Or do you have the type of customer who is punching the clock and who completes the minimum amount of activities required to get through the day and pass the annual review?

Determining where your customer fits in this subset is important. Let me give you an example from my field of sales training. In years past, when time and funding were more abundant, many regional managers and directors of training would seek new ways to improve upon the skills of their salespeople. They would be receptive to new ideas and express a willingness to pilot a new course to determine their effectiveness. For the most part, once they experienced one of our sessions, they would continue with an expanded application of our content. In this case, the training department would explore what was available and make selections on these topics based on their impact. In today's environment of downsizing and increased demand on individuals, departments' time, and resources, the same spirit of discovery is not prevalent. No longer will the training department initiate or be receptive to new ideas if the "C" level (executive level) is not requesting it. Think about the people you are meeting. Are they just trying to get through the day or are they willing to take the time? If you are lucky enough to be on their "to do" list, things will move forward. But if not, you can expect a prolonged delay in getting your ideas and products or services accepted.

## How Do You Get Through the Day?

How about you? Are you just trying to get through your day? With each category of customer, there is a corresponding frequency of preparation.

If you are calling on your more frequent customers, those who buy a lot of what you are selling, you probably are seeing these customers more often. The question has to be raised: Are you preparing for these customers with greater effort? Such a customer might be one that you see every week, every other week, or every third week. This is the type of customer who might also have others from your organization calling on him or her. So, when you are not able to be there, someone else will be! Even though your relationship may be established, greater effort is required to create interesting discussions to present fresh and unique ideas. If you don't there is a possibility that this customer will give you limited time, unless you can really create an impact during your visit.

Unfortunately, this may also be the type of customer you see so often and prepare for the least, because you are running a mile a minute. Did you ever pull up in the customer's parking lot, sit in your car, and say to yourself as you are reading your call notes, "What am I going to do today? I was just here last week!" Wow, guess what? This could be exactly how your customers think about you when they see you walking down the hallway or into their workspace! The customer just saw you last week and is wondering what you could possibly have to say that is worth taking up time and fitting into a crowded schedule.

If these are the thoughts that are going through your customers' minds, there is a need to break the monotony and better connect with them to create an increased level of receptivity. Whether your frequency with a customer is once a day, a couple of times a week, or only a few times a year, you need to create excitement during each of your contacts, regardless of whether they are face-to-face or on the phone. Certainly the frequent customer is going to be the biggest challenge in this regard.

You need to ask yourself whether the customer regards you as a welcome face, whether a customer wants to see you when you walk down the hall, or does that customer want to turn down the next corner and run away? That may be a tough question to answer; however, if the answer is the latter, we have a little work to do. Think back to your experiences in school or at some of your prior jobs. When you saw a particular person walking toward you, did you alter your path? Did you happen to duck into the restroom or focus on your BlackBerry to look busy? Does your customer act the same way when you approach?

## What Is Your Plan?

Later in this book, we will talk about creating a map for moving relationships forward and closing. Part of the map or plan is to determine the number of steps it takes to convert a nonuser of your product or service into an advocate. Another part of the map or equation is how often you see the customer and what needs to take place at every contact.

Determining and completing this task will increase the interest level of the customer and will reignite your approach for every call. After each contact, the customer should feel that the communication was beneficial, enlightening, and stimulating, and should be willing to spend time with you again. And you, in turn, should feel encouraged to go back and see them again.

So how many times do you see your customer in a year? Do you see your customer twice a year, twice a month, or twice a week? I would like you to keep that number in mind and also give consideration to the estimated number of contacts your customer receives from the individuals you are competing against.

## Does This Sound Familiar?

Let's just say that you're seeing your customer once a week—about 50 times a year. Your customer might see up to five other sales reps just like you. That would be five times 50 or a total of 250 times a year that a customer is hearing nearly the same story. Since we are focusing on the frequent customer, he or she probably has heard some version of your story numerous times and has heard your competition's story just as often. The problem is that the stories are starting to run together. In the next chapter, you will be introduced to the term *schema*. This term provides insight on how a customer makes a decision.

There is a need to remember that your customer is hearing pretty much the same stuff from several other salespeople who compete against you several times a week and multiple times a month. The record needs to be broken. The pattern needs to be stopped. This is the customer that has a good understanding of what your product or service can do. This is the customer that you probably need to get "out of the box," the customer you need to free from any predisposed thinking. But up to this point, this might be the customer who sees you blending into the wallpaper, who hardly even notices you. Think about yourself. What happens when someone calls you at home to solicit for a product or service—do you hang up or listen? When my office receives a call about how we like our long-distance service or the office supplies we recently ordered, the standard reply we give is that we are satisfied. Essentially what we are saying is that because we are satisfied with what we are currently getting, we don't feel a need or compulsion to take the time to decide to change vendors. The only time that a renewed level of interest or attention happens is when a problem arises. Regrettably, you cannot rely on the other guy failing. As a high-level salesperson, it is your responsibility to make things happen. This is what we are going to talk about in this book: how to make things happen more often.

Let's move on to the next category, the occasional customer. Occasional customers are less likely to be guilty of "just trying to get through the day." Because this is an occasional purchase, the focus and attention will be greater. Chances are the customer will be hearing many types of presentations for the first time. There is less of a chance of repetition and duplication. This type of customer will usually listen intently to every presentation and is less likely to have already formed many preconceived opinions and biases about your product or service. There will be less of a chance of a deep-rooted incumbent to make the process more difficult.

The occasional customer gets a lot of attention at the onset. This is the person, department, or company who is going to make a decision that will strongly affect the direction of the department and possibly the company as a whole. The decisions that will be made will probably have effects that last for a long time. Therefore, your effort and coordination of resources will need to be more detailed. This sales scenario will demand a more comprehensive approach that identifies all of the players, the obstacles, strengths, and weaknesses. A team effort involving you and others from your organization will most likely be required.

At the beginning, the occasional customer has not yet set in concrete his or her opinions, and has not yet developed favorites. This is the customer category in which the playing field is the most evenly set. With good preparation and execution, the occasional customer can be developed into a better customer. The only caution that is needed when dealing with customers in this category is if an incumbent product or service is present, the situation, issues, and rules for the frequent user are also appropriate for this customer category.

The moderate user is the user who has familiarity with your product or service but is not overburdened by an overabundance of contacts. The moderate user is likely to be knowledgable about some of your products or services but not all of them. These moderate users may be good, regular users of one of your products or services but not of the others you offer. The moderate user is the customer category that may have room for growth. For example, if we are looking at the world of investment, the customer might be investing in a bond fund that you are offering but may not yet have diversified into other types of investments. This customer has not put money into equities or real estate, areas about which he or she may only have limited knowledge, and therefore might be willing to explore the viability of such options.

If you have several customers that fit in the moderate user category, I suggest that this should be the first group of customers for you to attack. In a sense, the low-hanging fruit is not gone.

Conversely, the frequent user has already picked the lower half of the tree clean, and it will take a lot of work and effort to get more business because of the preexisting biases and schemas (more on that in the next chapter). Strategically a choice needs to be made as to where you want to get more business. On the other hand, the moderate user is open to growth and expansion. If there is a drawback in this category, it is because of the lack of contact on your part. Customers in this category may have a "stepchild" mindset. But with renewed attention and quality contacts, such feelings can get erased.

# Plan of Action

Let's put this process into action. To begin with, you need to focus on who your customers are and attempt to categorize them in terms of how often you call on them and how interested they presently are in what you have to offer them.

## Compiling a Customer List

Your first step is to compile a list of all of your customers and indicate the category to which each of them belongs: frequent, moderate, or occasional. See Table 1.1. If a customer is categorized as frequent, you would place a checkmark (✓) in the blank gray subcolumn under the "Frequent" heading. If a customer is moderate, place a checkmark in the blank gray subcolumn under the "Moderate" heading. If a customer is occasional, place a checkmark in the blank gray subcolumn under "Occasional." Your list may be longer, depending on how large your customer base is, but the basic format to use is as shown here.

| Customer name | Customer category and level of commitment | | | | | |
|---|---|---|---|---|---|---|
| | Frequent | | Moderate | | Occasional | |
| | + | – | + | – | + | – |
| | + | – | + | – | + | – |
| | + | – | + | – | + | – |
| | + | – | + | – | + | – |
| | + | – | + | – | + | – |

TABLE 1.1  Customer list

## Assigning a Level of Interest

Once you have categorized each of your customers in your list in terms of how much and often they purchase your product or service, you need to take a further look at the customer subset. Is a customer you approach just trying to get through the day or is that customer interested in learning more and improving on what they are doing? You might categorize a customer's level of interest as either "Caring" (indicating a greater level of interest and a willingness to learn about alternative products or services to make their department or process better) or "Getting by" (indicating a lesser level of present interest in the products or services you are offering. If a customer is caring, circle the + sign in the subcolumn under that customer's category. If a customer is just getting by, circle the – sign in the subcolumn under that customer's category. If a customer falls in the middle, don't circle the + or –, thereby indicating a medium level of interest.

# How Does Familiarity Affect Your Customer's Level of Interest?

The final area in assessing your customer's interest is their familiarity with your story? Is your customer very familiar with it or with that of your competitors? If your story is different from that of your competitors, would this make a difference on how the customer selects a product or service? Is there a 90 percent chance that a customer has heard your story, or is the probability much lower? Taking into consideration the degree of familiarity, make an overall determination of the customer's receptivity, as represented in the table by circling the plus (+) or minus (−) subcolumn in the appropriate category.

In sum, each customer should be categorized both in terms of how often you have been calling on them for purchases *and* in terms of their present level of interest. Considering these factors together will help you determine how to approach them.

Once you have completed this process, you have provided an estimate of the likelihood of each customer's interest level, whether it is strong, intermediate, or low. You have made an initial prediction as to the customer's willingness to listen and receptivity to change. Obviously, this is not a foolproof method that would allow you to accurately determine the exact interest level of every customer in every situation, since people (and situations) can sometimes be unpredictable, but it will help you to decide where to attack first.

During many of my live training sessions, I share with the participants the concepts and content you are about to receive on how to move some of your customers forward. You won't always succeed in this, but this book is about moving a select few of your customers forward. In the business world, moving only a select few forward is what makes the difference between having a mediocre year and getting the award at the national sales meeting. Let's read on and see if we can help you get that award!

# 2

# Schema:
# Is It Happening to You?

Faced with making a decision, people frequently try to remember how they did things in the past. They will take into consideration their thoughts, feeling, intentions, and past experiences to make their choice. During that process, they will reflect back and use their memory to reveal any prior patterns, methods, or previous decision-making processes to assist them in moving forward. In a sense, we as individuals have somewhat of an autobiographical memory to help us come to a conclusion.

How about you—do you think about how you do things? Do you remember the outcome as well as the process you went through to make a decision? If you do, do you ask yourself if the process is worth repeating? For instance, what are your methods when it comes to buying a new or used car? Do you research the Internet for the most up-to-date reports on the car's safety and maintenance history? Do you test drive the car and compare it to others in the same category? Or do you buy it because it just feels right or you think you are getting a good deal? How do you go about buying something that is a little bigger and more permanent, such as a house? There is a good chance you will visit many "open houses" and pour through report after report before you decide to buy a house. You probably will not buy the first home you see. Both of these decisions require an analysis; however, the car-buying process may happen more often in one's life and you may not be as thorough in your analysis as you would be for the purchase of a home. Familiarity and frequency will influence the way a person buys a product or service. With respect to the purchase of a car, you might buy or lease an automobile every few years. So, for most people, the process of car-buying has more familiarity and frequency than buying a house. The more frequent and familiar, the more habits and predisposed notions are present. If you happen to be a fan of purchasing an American-made car, the foreign car salesperson has his work cut out for him. The American car salesperson has an advantage because of the habits, otherwise known as "schemas" that are present.

Now let's look at your product or service. How often does the person you are calling on purchase what you have to sell? Is it daily, weekly, monthly, or only every several years when the contract is up? Is the customer a frequent, moderate, or occasional user? These factors certainly play a role in the selection process of your product or service and have an impact on the person's purchasing habits.

## Making a Decision

Let's think about some of the choices you may have faced in your life. These choices can span from the very serious—should

I change my college major, relocate, take a new job, or get married—to the not-so-serious—whom should I choose for my fantasy football team? Obviously, all but the last of the above
decisions would have a great deal of impact on your life. But
how often have we looked back after we made the decision and
questioned why it was so difficult? There is a good possibility
that the vision and decision were not clear at the time. There
were unresolved issues, uncertainty, and doubt. These are some
of the elements that go into making a decision and cause a
decision to be delayed or put off. For the most part, the person
did not have a habit or ritual available to help make a decision.
The decision process was new, with no history or decision tree
to rely upon.

The same is true when a customer buys a product or service.
Your customers may have the same concerns, especially if they
have not previously purchased what you are selling. Let's refer
back to a couple of the things that I just mentioned. Leaving
marriage out of the mix, you can look back and determine without hesitation that moving, taking the new job, choosing your
college and major, or picking the correct running back or point
guard for your fantasy team was a good or bad decision. But at
the time, it was a difficult choice. Why? Because it may not have
aligned with your habits, knowledge, or the technical term called
*schema*. For the most part, once the decision has been made and
executed, it is clear whether the choice was correct. And now
there is a pattern or process that can be called upon to help make
the next decision. The key in selling is to make the customer
comfortable, break his/her schema, and try something different
from your usual product or service. If a customer is a first-time
buyer, you should help craft the schema; if a customer is a frequent or moderate buyer of your competition's product or service, you need to break that schema.

## How the Customer
## Thinks

All of us have an autobiographical memory that we call upon when we make a decision. We think about the past to give us an indication of whether the decision we are about to make (in the future) will be a good choice. Will the decision, based on my current knowledge, be accurate and reflect well upon me, my work, or my project? The customer fears making a wrong decision that would cause a setback or maybe even negatively affect his or her status.

Remembering this information about your customers provides insights into their personal histories and contributes to understanding how they arrive at decisions. This is especially pertinent if the customer is a frequent user of your product or service and can recall an in-depth history of his/her experiences. The term "neuroassociation" has been given to this circumstance. For example, when you were younger, you may have burned your finger or hand on the stove. Once this happens, you remember not to put your hand or finger where it can be burned again. The same could be said when your customer makes a decision. Did the customer have a good or bad experience with the purchase of a particular product or service? Or does he/she have a track record with your company? If he/she did have a bad experience, it will certainly be more difficult moving him/her forward and changing the way he/she thinks. Uncovering customers' predisposition or history can help you to get a sense of understanding of how they will react to things in the future, that is, how they go about making decisions. In the upcoming chapters you will be introduced to several skills that will allow you to accomplish this task and uncover this information.

# How We Make Decisions

A schema (which can be different for every person) is how some-one processes new information, tries to make sense out of infor-mation, and comes to a decision. Your goal is to be aware of the customer's schema and use it to your advantage.

To better explain schema, I researched several sources and found numerous articles that can help explain this process. In an article titled "Schema Theory," by Robert Axelrod of the Uni-versity of California, Berkeley, Axelrod explains that "the world is complex, and that a person's schema allows them to make sense out of it" (*American Political Science Review*, 1973).

How do people make a decision, especially if it is difficult or complex? According to Axelrod, "One of the most important tools that people use is a schema." A schema is a "pre-existing assumption about the way the world is organized." When new information becomes available (such as your sales presentation for a product or service), the person (the customer) tries to fit the new information into the pattern that he or she has used in the past to interpret the information about the same situation. If the new information does not fit very well, something has to give.

Erin N. Procacci, Ph.D., is a licensed psychologist. She earned her graduate degrees from George Washington Univer-sity and the University of Miami. Currently, she works at Nova Southeastern University on a SAMHSA-funded grant and is an adjunct faculty member in the Center for Psychological Studies. Dr. Procacci has worked with hundreds of individuals across a variety of settings, many of whom were faced with very difficult choices. When asked about how people in business make deci-sions, she stated that there are various models that can help in our understanding the decision-making process. For instance, rational decision-making models involve a number of cognitive processes in which each step in the process follows a logical and sequenced order. If the businessperson is thorough in his method of selection, he will analyze several possible alternatives prior to arriving at his decision. The final decision the individual arrives at is assumed to be the one she views as the best possible outcome and comes with the greatest probability of occurring.

Dr. Procacci suggested that many theories of decision making draw from cognitive psychology and stress the importance of psychological aspects of the decision-making process, namely, the importance of schemas. *Schemas are mental frameworks that help individuals to organize knowledge and experience and to provide a platform from which to interpret and process new information.* Individuals develop schemas for everything. This includes using schemas to develop scripts for action. A script for action is a preset, stereotyped chain of actions that define a familiar or recurrent situation. Schemas become embedded habits that affect how a customer might interpret new information, and thus, how decisions are made. Once the customer forms specific schemas, they are difficult to change. Dr. Procacci acknowledged that this may contribute to why salespeople experience difficulty getting customers to consider new and different purchases. Even with repeated visits and multiple communications about a new product or service, unless the salesperson can trigger a discussion that challenges the customer's current schema and associated scripts for action, change in the selection or purchasing decisions is either unlikely or delayed.

According to schema theory, change is relative to the amount of new information that is encountered.

As customers are exposed to new information, they may incorporate this new information into their schemas. This could lead to a modified or new decision-making process. When a request is made to a customer, it is important for the salesperson to assess (to the extent possible) what the customer's current schemas are with regard to the request at hand. In addition, the salesperson should realize that the information presented needs to be novel enough that it challenges the customer's current related schemas and is worth evaluating. For example, if the salesperson is asking the same boring questions and giving the same boring presentation, the possibility of the customer's schema being altered or changed is remote.

The customer's schemas are activated when they are asked to make a decision. When this occurs, the customer will filter back to determine if a schema comes to mind. For example, when was the last time the customer made this type of decision or how often has the customer made this type of decision? Is the selection process fresh in the customer's mind or would he have difficulty accessing what he did in the past? According to Dr. Procacci, if the associated schemas are readily accessible, those schemas will be used as a cognitive shortcut for interpreting the new information. She goes on to say that another important element in decision making is heuristics, which are the rules individuals use to test their schemas and the processing of new information. In certain cases, the customer's rules or heuristics can lead to biases toward the decision-making process. If this is the case, the customer might rely too much, or "anchor," on past experiences and might be unwilling or unable to look beyond the scope of past experiences and to reject the unfamiliar.

Nick Martino is a vice president and general manager of ITW (Illinois Tool Works) in Chicago. ITW is a multinational manufacturer of a diversified range of value-adding and short lead-time industrial products and equipment. The company consists of approximately 840 business units in 57 countries and employs approximately 59,000 people.

When Martino was asked about his schema, his answer was somewhat unusual: "With respect to my decision-making processes, I am always searching for the next great innovation, need, or resource that can help the group move away from common ground and their comfort zone. I recognize the process of schema, and I am always questioning why we continue to do business with the same suppliers year in and year out." Martino goes on to say, "When we do break out from a known source, the standard we use to move forward is normally based on innovation. It is rare that we move on raw materials suppliers because we would need to do formulation changes, retesting, and qualification for getting the product reapproved—but when a supplier has taken the initiative to show us the outcomes of pretesting trials and successes, which is what it would take to make us change, I am willing to spend the money to research it further. What is usually very interesting in this model for changing schemas is that we do not normally change based on a lower price—this is the last part of our focus. What is commonly the driver is that we change because of a process improvement—the ability to be more environmentally compliant, the ability to "sell a story" that will differentiate us is in the marketplace.

## Selling a Story

Let's take a look at some simple decisions we make during the course of our daily lives. Let's focus on three areas: clothes, cars, and entertainment. When it comes to caring for our clothes, we generally take our clothes to the same dry cleaners. We might initially make the choice of where to take our clothes to be cleaned because of the location of the store. It might be easy for us to swing by and drop off or pick up. Maybe we select the cleaners because it has a great special on shirts. Somewhere along the way, the price or location contributes to our patronage of a certain dry cleaner. But what happens if the cleaner ruins a shirt? If it gives you a credit and continues to treat you correctly, you will keep going back. Suppose the cleaner moves a couple of blocks or discontinues the shirt special? The pattern is changed! The information that was used to interpret your selection of the dry cleaner has changed. You can't rely on the same information from the past to carry your decision-making process forward. It looks like it might be a time for change because your schema has been altered. At this time, you are open to other dry cleaners and are willing to start the process over again.

How about the other two choices: cars and entertainment? For the most part we take our car to the same mechanic. There is a good chance that we go to the dealership where we purchased the car. The convenience of using the dealership and its "certified" parts often compels us to keep using it, especially if a free loaner is provided and the car is under warranty. But what happens when you need to buy new tires? And what happens when the warranty expires? Chances are the schema is imbedded so strongly that you keep going back to the dealership and don't go to your local mechanic.

The last choice is entertainment, specifically your favorite restaurant. I imagine you have eaten in many restaurants over the years, perhaps some local and others across state lines. If you travel, you might have eaten in the biggest dives or some of the more elegant places in the country, consuming both memorable and forgettable meals. I like to keep the more memorable meals in mind and erase the bad ones. But for all of us, we probably have our favorite restaurant, which may have been introduced to us by friends or recommended by something that we read or heard. In any event, whether it was through trial and error or a referral, we landed at the place we like to go for our special night out. I know that this is the case for me. My wife and I have our special place in the suburbs of Philadelphia (a great city for food!). I have my favorites around the country as well, but my favorite hometown place is where we spend many if not all of our special occasions.

Over the years, I have taken a poll of the customers and students I work with, asking more than a thousand people if they have a favorite restaurant. Out of all of the people I have asked, all but a few responded, "Yes, I absolutely have a favorite restaurant." Once I learn that they have a favorite place, I then ask: "Do you order the same type of food when you go there?" The almost unanimous answer is *yes*! Same place, same food. There you have it! Okay, by now you may have realized that this same person who is going to her favorite restaurant is your customer. Using her schema, she selected "her" place, and not until she has a series of bad meals and or service will this change. This creates a problem if you are not the incumbent. We cannot wait for the other company to make a mistake!

For the most part, the customer wants balance. We like balance in our personal and professional world. According to Axelrod, we want a balanced set of friends, and we look for a certain set of criteria in our friends. Once those criteria are met, the relationship begins. Axelrod also suggests that, in some cases, the circle of friends can be expanded. For example, friends of friends are acceptable; much like enemies of friends would be rejected. If we think about it, this plays into the notion of the importance of referrals with business. If one client likes our work, that should influence others positively.

In the business world, a customer who receives new information about a topic or project tries to fit the new information into an existing interpretation. If the new information fits well, there is no problem. However, if it does not fit exactly, the customer has a variety of tactical choices. The customer can try to use the same schema with the same interpretations. If this occurs, there is a good chance that this decision process will require some form of discounting of the new (discrepant) information. Or an entirely new schema will be needed to allow the customer to process the decision and select your product or service.

Since a schema is about how a customer observes and makes sense of a complex decision, you will be better off than your competition if you can learn the customer's schema, but this will not be simple. Therefore, the clearer and easier you connect to the customer with your ideas and presentation, the better they will resonate with the customer and the more likely it is that you will get a sale. So let's look into how people make a decision and how we can break or change their habits and schemas.

## The Customer's Perspective

Mike Capaldi is a senior executive at one of the world's largest pharmaceutical companies. I posed a couple of questions to him about the issue of access and breaking a customer's schema.

Capaldi suggests that the biggest problem is the frequency of communications that he receives on a daily basis: "The overload has gotten so great that I have had to set up a process that allows me to even consider a vendor's offering. On average, I receive between 15 and 20 e-mails a day, and they are not all spam." He continues, "I get a dozen or so phone calls per week. In some cases, the offering interests me; however, it takes a lot of effort to invest the time to research them." Compounding this issue,

Capaldi reports that initially many of the offerings duplicate those that he's already received. "That's not to say that there aren't better products out there," he says, "but if I feel like our needs are being met by a vendor-partner, the likelihood of a switch really minimizes the chances of us working together." In this situation, Capaldi sees no need to break his schema.

When I questioned Capaldi about how he ultimately chooses someone to talk with, knowing that many people are trying to reach him, he replied, "If the offering is unique and fills an unmet need, I will initiate formal contact. In some cases, referrals drive who I would spend time researching. For most, they are unable to get past the face-to-face stage, because they fail to identify what my true needs are and how their product or service can meet those needs."

## How a Customer Makes a Decision

Let's examine Capaldi's comments. From a scientific point of view, the decision-making process starts when customers receive information about a new product or service. The first question that customers will ask themselves is whether there is already a similar product or service in place. Have I made this decision before? If there is information about the decision from a prior project, the next question is, "How does the new information that I am receiving fit into my existing interpretations?" If it is a good fit, there is a probable reason to move forward. However, if there is a disconnect between the new product or service and the existing one, then blame is affixed by comparing the credibility of the source of the new product or service with the confidence of the existing product or service. If the search process (sales calls and presentations) fails to find a schema which provides a sufficiently good fit, the new product or service is discounted and the process ends.

## The Decision Tree

Before making a decision, the customer evaluates all available information in a process that usually unfolds like this:

**Decision Tree**

1. Is there a current product or service already available?
2. How does the new product or service compare with the already existing one?
3. If there is a need to evaluate, the decision to investigate is made with little or no hesitation.
4. If there is no apparent benefit arising from the new product or service, the customer assigns blame to the credibility of the new source.
5. Can the new source overcome the blame and credibility gap to move forward?
6. If the gap cannot be closed, the decision is to remain with the status quo (the existing product or service).

I admit this is a lot to digest, but this thought process is what is getting in the way of your closing more sales and moving more relationships forward. Let's break the process down into simpler terms.

## Breaking Down the Process

Step by step, the process unfolds as shown in Figure 2.1.

Step 1: Customer receives information from a sales presentation.

Step 2: Customer processes the new information as to how well it fits with what the customer already knows.

Step 3: Is it a good presentation that aligns with prior selection criteria? If so, the sale process moves forward.

Step 3A: If the sales presentation does not align, the customer scrutinizes you and your presentation for viability.

Step 3B:  The salesperson revises and edits the presentation to
          address the gaps in credibility.
Step 4:  The sales process is completed.

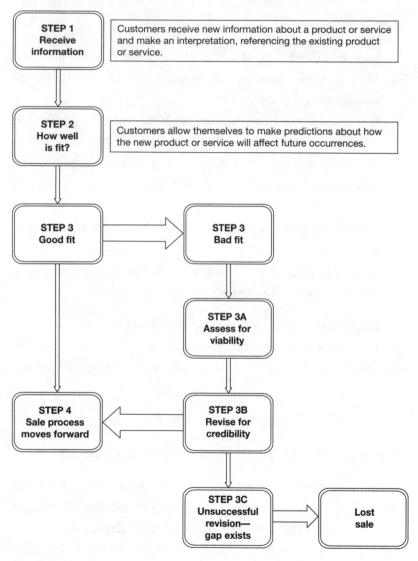

**FIGURE 2.1**  Flowchart of the four steps of the decision-making process.

If there is no prior experience or interpretation of the new project, there is no past history involved in the decision. Therefore, there is no schema, no habit, or any roadblocks from past experiences. If this is the case, your only concern is how to move forward and be credible. If we refer back to the categories that are introduced in Chapter 1, this is the customer who has very little experience with your product or service. The formula just mentioned would have a predominant role for the frequent or moderate customer who is buying from your competition.

The four-step decision-making process is how the customer makes a selection. To be successful in this process, great attention needs to be focused on your ability to ensure that your "new information" connects and improves upon his or her "old information." To make this occur, a new level of dialogue is suggested in the upcoming chapters. The key in moving the relationship forward is to make sure that customers do not get the feeling that their past decisions are coming under attack.

If the customer has the feeling that what she did in the past is inadequate according to your standards, she will dig in her heels and magnify any concern she might have about your credibility. If this occurs, the likelihood of a sale is remote. The following is another way of looking at this process:

1. A customer receives new information and makes an interpretation, referencing the existing information.
2. A customer allows himself to make predictions about how the new information will affect future occurrences.
3. A customer will interpret the new information as to how well it fits the "gaps" that were identified.
4. A customer reflects upon his existing schema and determines the credibility of the new information and source.

## Moving Forward

According to a paper by Pieters, Baumgartner, and Bagozzi ("Biased Memory for Prior Decision Making," *Organizational Behavior and Human Decision Processes* 99, 2006, pp. 34–48), "there is a growing stream of research on memory for specific mental states in decision making, such as attitudes, emotions, partner and self-evaluations, and especially predictions."

A customer will revisit her memory for performance of a project or product selection that was or was not used in the past. If the outcome of trying something new worked well, it is safe to assume that the person you are speaking with is predisposed to new or different ideas. On the other hand, if a person experienced a bad outcome, even if it wasn't dealing with a product or service that you provide, this negative association for going "out of the box" could impede your progress in getting that customer to do something different. Technically, one's predictions about the outcomes of an event are often systematically influenced by one's knowledge about the actual outcomes (i.e., outcome knowledge), a phenomenon termed the "hindsight bias."

In sports, this is referred to as Monday morning quarterbacking, meaning that it is easy to see what went wrong *after* the game is played and the outcome determined.

## Blame Game

Sales professionals should be aware that all these elements influence the customer's decision-making process, bringing us to what we call the blame game. The blame game is how customers validate their decision to change. If the blame game occurs, it can lean in your favor, putting you in a better position for making a sale. Do you recognize the following components of the blame game?

1.  New information is a bad fit for the existing or old interpretation.
2.  The new information is judged as fairer and more documented and comes from a more credible source than existing information.
3.  The new information creates a claim that there are discrepancies in the old information.
4.  When the old information is blamed, the old schema is revised to reflect support for the new information.

In a nutshell, this is how we get a customer to change! This is your goal when dealing with the frequent, moderate, and occasional customers. Sometimes, there will be limited circumstances supporting the existing schema that will be beneficial. This occurs when your "new information" fits well into the existing information. When this occurs, the customer feels that the information is a good fit and is judged as persuasive and accurate.

## Summary

A schema is one of the most important tools that a person uses to make a decision. A schema, in lay terms, is how a person reflects back to prior experiences to help them make a decision in the future. Clearly the schemas of a Democrat and a Republican will be different. To each, his schema is correct. The challenge is how to communicate with both sides.

When information about a topic becomes available, a person tries to fit the new information into the pattern used in the past to interpret information about the same situation and move forward. If the new information does not fit very well, something has to change. If the information fits, things are fine. Balance is an important element of commonly used schemas. Balance for a customer provides a view of things in black and white. Balance can be defined in terms of no more than two objects—positive and negative; essential and desired. When a customer gets new information, he tries to fit it into the old interpretation. If the new information fits into the previously held opinions and experiences, there is no problem. If the new information doesn't fit, the customer will try to use the same schema, which means that the new suggestion (your product or service) will not appear to be the best fit. The customer will need to be convinced that an entirely new schema is in order.

Getting customers to move to a new schema can be accomplished. It refers back to the same scenario that was discussed earlier about relocating, taking the new job, or deciding where to go to school. The challenge is to get the customer to let go of the old schema or habit and accept a new one.

# 3

# What Keeps
# You from Getting
# More Business?

Before we discuss the actual skills that will enable you to move existing relationships forward and create new relationships, I would like to explore one other element that affects the sales process. I have introduced the concept of schema to enable you to understand how people make decisions. This concept also enables us to identify why initiatives will slow down, become dormant, and eventually fail.

Another huge reason why we don't get more business is you, the salesperson. This is a difficult thing to share because you have been selling for years, earning a living, and developing relationships. It is not the product, service, pricing, or availability of the product or service that holds you back. In this chapter I explore why some people can sell exactly the same product or service with success and others cannot.

## How We Are
## Taught to Sell

Frequency, attentiveness, and knowledge can play key roles in assisting you to obtain and gain more business. There is a need to explore more than these three areas. Allow me to give you an example. Let's return for a moment to childhood. When you were a child, if someone gave you a balloon and asked you to pop it, I am guessing that many of you reading this book would grab that balloon and start poking it with your finger. The more you poked, the greater the likelihood of your success at breaking and deflating the balloon. In a sense, as an adult salesperson, that is what we still do. Every day, week, bimonthly, or monthly, we show up at the customer's office and poke him for more business. The more we poke, the better the chance of increasing sales. However, somewhere along the way, all that poking begins to bruise a couple of customers.

In some cases, our past successes and complacency have played a role in our inability to evolve to the next level as a salesperson. Sales professionals could take a page from an athlete's playbook, because athletes practice. For example, football, basketball, and tennis players who play their sport growing up may attend a couple of sports summer camps. If they are good, they get to start for their high school teams. They practice for days before playing a game. If a player is good enough to advance to the next level, he gets recruited. More practice takes place at the collegiate level: spring practice, summer leagues, and camp, followed by days of drills and more practice. Finally the season comes around, and more practice and games occur. This pattern repeats over four years. After college, an athlete may hope to get drafted as a professional player, where he will find more camps and more practice! For years, athletes work on their game, perfecting the basics and working on improving their skills and techniques to become more proficient at the highest level.

Now let's take a look at the world of professional selling. You may have seen a television commercial that is run during college sporting events that portrays college athletes playing various sports: swimming, track and field, basketball, volleyball, or softball. The commercial depicts each athlete on and off the court, pool, or field, both in their uniforms and in business attire. The commercial's message is that not all of us go pro in sports; in fact, almost all of us will go pro in something else. If you are reading this book, you made the decision to go pro in selling.

## Pursuing Excellence

Whether you were involved in sports, music, theater, or perhaps painting, reading, writing, or volunteerism, the ongoing pursuit of excellence required time and practice. When we were students, we spent time studying, but we were eager to have fun outside the classroom. Most of these pastimes required practice to become good and a lot of practice to become really good.

Allow me to share with you an extreme experience. As I mentioned earlier, when I first entered into the profession of sales education, I became involved with an established sales training company. I was the student who was mentored by the individuals who sold me the training program. When I joined the company, I shadowed the teachers for nearly a year as they presented the program. After a year, I felt ready to lead the class on my own. For the most part, things went well. At the time, I also realized there was a need to surround myself with other staff members to make up for my youth and relative inexperience.

The additional staff members either had more sales experience than I or brought a specific skill into the classroom, including a writing expert, a psychologist, a clothing expert, a telemarketing executive, and so on. As the reins were handed over to me, I started going out in the world to make sales calls. I would call on medium-to-large organizations to generate interest in enrolling their salespeople in my seminars. Some of the customers I called on had prior experience with my firm's sales training program and were receptive to enrolling more of their salespeople into the course.

Eventually, I made a pivotal sales call on one of the larger banks in the Philadelphia area. I was meeting with the head of training and development, and the call was going well. I was following the classic sales model that was taught to me during my attendance at the sales training course. However, something unexpected happened. The director of training and development asked me what the course's experiential learning process was. I paused for a moment. I seemed to remember that this term meant how participants or students were taught. Confident that I understood the question, I replied, "We role-play after each skill is introduced." The training director looked right into my eyes and said, "You have no idea what I am talking about, do you?" Talk about an embarrassing moment (and I have had many over the years). I sank down in my chair, probably looked like a sheep, and said "I guess not." Needless to say, the sales call ended at that moment. I thanked her for her time and exited her office.

What a wake-up call! To be exact, it was a wake-up call that took about three years and many thousands of dollars to answer. Within a week of that sales call, I realized that there was another route for me to advance my knowledge of how to teach people. My research indicated that you could get a master's degree in adult education, otherwise known as training and development. At that moment, I made the choice to "go pro" in my profession. For the next three years, I attended classes that taught me how to design and present a training program. The courses were enlightening. As a matter of fact, one of my classes led to my first book, which I wrote many years ago.

But let me return to the person whom I met from the large bank. As you can imagine, I did not call her back for a follow-up appointment. I did, however, send her a follow-up note of appreciation for her candor and direction. Basically, I left the door open if, for some reason, I wanted to come back. I think you know where this story is heading. Guess whom I called the very week after I received my diploma. The training director accepted my call and scheduled an appointment to see me. You can imagine how anxious I was to tell my story. I think she was pretty surprised to hear about my transformation and the changes in my program. Interestingly enough, not long after that meeting, she decided to pursue a path outside banking. During that process, she joined my staff!

## The Sales Professional

Prior to attending graduate school, I listened to as many sales tapes as possible. I attended at least one sales training program every three months and read countless books on the topic. I continued to develop my talents and skills in selling, but still something was missing.

I wasn't sure what it was at the time, but after many years of selling, conducting classes, and meeting salespeople, I finally realized what it was.

## *Personal Branding*

As you enter a company, you are taught about the industry and its products and services. You are required to know your stuff. In some companies and industries, you have to pass a test to enter the world of professional selling. This is particularly true with real estate, finance, and the world of pharmaceutical sales. In real estate and finance, you need a license. In pharmaceutical sales, you need to pass the test to prove your knowledge of the drugs you are selling and the diseases that they address.

You pass the test; now you are certified. You are certified just like thousands of others in your industry. As Mike Capaldi is quoted as saying in Chapter 2, dozens of salespeople try to cross his path and get a chance to meet him. Only a select few get the opportunity. The ones who do are unique; they have "a way" about them. They have personal branding.

Referring back to the story about the balloon, you can keep poking at the balloon. Eventually some of the balloons will pop; maybe most will not. Personal branding is one of the elements that will enable you to throw the dart at the balloon to get better results.

### *What Do You Select to Help You Stand Out?*

What do you need to do to stand out from the rest? On occasion I will have former athletes or entertainers participate in one of my classes. It is novel to hear about their experiences, and most people are interested to hear about their lives in the world of professional sports or entertainment. But once the story is told, they too are students in my class, just like the rest of the salespeople. If you happen to be somewhat unusual and have a "past life" that is more interesting than most of us, that could be your initial branding. There is a good chance that you will get through the door if your name is recognizable. But most of us don't have that, and even if we do, we need to be able to back it up once we do get through the door.

### Determining Your Personal Branding

Your branding process can and most certainly will evolve over the years. The first step is to identify the need for "your brand." I would like to take you through a process that I experienced. It first started with a mentor on how to sell. That at least got me into the game. It evolved through education. After the completion of my graduate studies, I had the good fortune to write a book. As a sales trainer, I have to compete with hundreds of companies and individuals who do the same thing I do. Writing a book opened a few more doors, because I could be introduced as an author; however, the breakthrough didn't occur till several years later.

Some years ago, I had the opportunity to participate in the Peter Lowe Success Tour seminars. These were one-day events held in major cities across the country at major indoor arenas. The venues would typically be the places where the city's professional basketball team or top entertainment acts would perform.

You can imagine the excitement and challenge that was ahead of me. I had an opportunity to speak in front of 20,000 to 30,000 people at one time. Then it hit me, "Oh my gosh. I have to speak in front of how many people?!" Once I realized what I had gotten myself into, I contacted the Peter Lowe group for some suggestions. I asked, "What is the most important thing I should do on stage?" The answer was quite simple: "Make sure you connect with your audience." I paused for a second and said, "How do I connect with an audience when I don't even know what they are selling and where they come from?" Their answer was, "That's why we pay you the big bucks" (well not really). I asked them to point me in the right direction to accomplish that task. They suggested that I should hire a coach. I took their advice and hired one. Let's reflect back: college education, mentor in sales, master's degree, and now a coach. It was not a cheap proposition. This coach was expensive, but I will admit it was worth the money. She taught me how to connect with my audience.

## Connecting with Your Audience

I had spent thousands of dollars and dedicated hours of preparation to get ready for this tour. Years before, while participating in college theater productions, I had learned that the rule of thumb was to practice at least 60 minutes for every 5 minutes you were on stage, just to get it right. My time slot on stage was approximately 45 minutes. Every day for almost three months I rehearsed the speech. I practiced the speech on the treadmill. Normally, I would run for just 30 minutes and be done with it, but the speech required an additional 15 minutes. Needless to say, I got in better shape.

My first speech was in Minneapolis at the Target Center. I arrived a day early to make sure all our shipments arrived and I was settled in. The night before the event, I was able to get access to the arena. As the maintenance crew preformed its last-minute steps to prepare for the next day's event, I ran through my speech several times. Many of the maintenance crew members smiled as they watched me present to an empty house and wished me good luck. I can still remember that rehearsal. The next day came, and it was my time to go on. You can imagine the butterflies in my stomach. As I waited backstage, I heard Peter complete my introduction. The lights were blinding, I couldn't see a thing. I flashed back to all of my rehearsals and started. About one minute into my speech, I shared my first story that talked about our ability or inability to communicate with our children. The audience roared with laughter. I connected! It seemed like the sounds of laughter were coming from all over. I found something that most of the audience could relate to. My story resonated with all the parents, aunts, and uncles in the audience. And even if the audience members didn't fit one of those categories, they really enjoyed the story.

So, that is it in a nutshell: *Connect with your audience.*

This is easier said than done. I went through quite the transformation. It was a change in perception. It was not all about the benefits and features of a product or service. As a matter of fact, in some cases, that is secondary. What is most important is how well you can connect with the individual on the other side of the desk.

I had spent thousands of dollars with a coach to realize that fact. Up to that point, I thought a good presentation would win people over. Not until that point of my evolution did I realize it was all about connecting. Your personal branding should focus on your ability to connect.

### How to Make a Connection

One profession that relies on connecting is the world of comedy. Why are some comedians so successful? It is because they connect with the audience's day-to-day lives. Stand-up comics make you laugh because they describe situations that have occurred in your life. They talk about something that you have done before—they connect with you. Successful television shows that depict family life describe situations that happen in normal and not-so-normal families. In a popular television show about three separate but related families that airs on a major network, the story lines harvest past family experiences. As I am laughing and watching the show, I think to myself, "Oh my gosh, this just happened to me; this is too funny!"

Connecting with your audience is a skill that takes time to develop. There are probably a couple of things you can do to determine how you can initially connect with your customer and eventually connect better than the incumbent supplier. The first step is to reach out to your current customers. Ask them why they buy from you. Chances are they will say that you provide a good product or service at a competitive price. They will also probably say that they can count on you if they need to get immediate attention. If you analyze that answer, that is pretty generic. That answer doesn't really help you learn why they selected you. There is no doubt that persistence pays off. I am a strong believer in being persistent with a purpose.

### Persistent with a Purpose

Persistent with a purpose is more than just calling a prospective client every couple of weeks. If you do that, you might be an annoyance. Persistence with a purpose is about creating a story that you know will connect and is worth driving home. I am not a big supporter of advertisements. If I like the product, I will buy it. However, I have to tell you where persistence with a purpose paid off. I am an avid exerciser. I can't say that I particularly like working out, but I know it is probably good for me in the long run. It allows me to eat the foods I like. I admit, however, that after a really good workout, I feel pretty good. I will also share with you that if I miss a workout, I feel guilty about it.

My work ethic is pretty strong when it comes to my profession and exercise. I don't need to be motivated; however, a product caught my attention not too long ago. Almost every day, while channel surfing to find a good sporting or poker event on television, I saw an infomercial about an exercise program. I listened to the person and watched the routine he would complete.

The infomercial lasted about 20 to 30 minutes, and I can't say I always watched the entire program. But these infomercials appeared on a regular basis, and when I met friends or colleagues who were using the program, I noticed how much better they looked. Finally, after months of repetitive exposures, I bought the program. It was one of the first things I ever bought from an infomercial.

The infomercial contained repetition with a strong and unique message. It spoke to me and connected with what I was missing in my workouts. The commercial asked, "Are you exercising and just going through the motions? Are you doing pretty much the same things every week without much improvement?" I hate to admit it, but I was saying, "Yes, yes, I am experiencing those issues." The commercial connected with me. It talked my language and identified my problems. It was different from the other commercials about similar exercise programs. I was converted after the first session. Now I am a zealot when it comes to this program.

**Connect with Your Customer**
1. Determine day-to-day challenges.
2. Create a story.
3. Reinforce the story, and drive it home.

*Converting Your Prospective Customer*
When I open up my live seminars and this book, one of the comments I make is that most people know how to sell and in certain circumstances have connected with their customers very well. I go on to say that the purpose of our effort is to help you connect with more of your customers. The purpose of this chapter is to introduce the idea of your personal branding. It is to enable you to start the process of learning what can make you

different. Your education and background can play a role in your distinction, but the overriding factor of why someone will choose you over other salespeople is your ability to connect.

### Starting the Connection Process

It might take some time to truly identify where or how you can connect with your prospective customers. What I have found to be most beneficial is if you can identify exactly what is happening in their day-to-day real world. Referring back to the exercise infomercial, it talked my language and identified how I was feeling about my exercise routine: It was boring, habitual, and regular. I wanted something a little different. That is your goal: Find out what the customer wants that is a little different.

### The Educated Guess

At first, you will have to guess at some of the issues that "keep your prospective customer up at night." After some trial and error, along with a little investigative work, you will determine a couple of areas that are in need of exploitation. Ask your prospective customer's assistant, associate, or worker bee what seems to be bogging down the process. What gets talked about or complained about the most? Get the details. If you learn this information, this is the stuff that goes into your introductory voice mail, e-mail, or any other communication. If your opening statements connect, you have a chance of getting better access than the other salesperson.

Validate the information you receive. Take the information you receive from one company or office and share it with others. Ask them how these situations compare to what they are seeing in their offices, processes, and day-to-day activities. The more validation you receive, the closer you get to connecting with the customer's day-to-day issues.

**Connect with Your Customer**

1. Determine day-to-day challenges.
2. Create a story.
3. Reinforce the story, and drive it home.

# Getting Started

Start the process by understanding that you, the salesperson, are the difference. At the outset, it is your approach, knowledge, and ability to connect that gets you in the game. Later on, your presentation will play a role in how you can accomplish what you need to accomplish. But first you need to focus on connecting and resonating with your prospective customer. To get an edge on the competition, you need to brand yourself. Your branding is how well you can connect with your audience. Just like my experience on the Peter Lowe Success Tour, it didn't click with me until I realized it wasn't about what I was selling or how good my presentation was; it was about them, the members of the audience.

The more you can identify with what a prospective customer is going through, the more you will appear to be the answer. At first you may misfire and identify a couple of wrong or insignificant issues. Don't worry about that. Simply ask the prospective customers, what seems to be an issue with them. Be undaunted. Keep up your notion of persistence with a purpose. You don't need to convert all your customers to advocates; you need to convert only a few to increase your success. When presenting the information that you obtained from your due diligence (which, may I add, never ends), serve it up to your customers in a very amenable style. Introduce your information in a way that the customer finds acceptable. My favorite way to introduce ideas is to determine their validity with the transition statement, "Chances are." Using "chances are" enables you to introduce the topic without an indictment. If the customer feels she is being attacked, she will shut down. If, however, your information is introduced in a subtle way, customers are receptive. The term "chances are" allows the customers to agree. If they don't agree, they can respond that it doesn't seem to happen to them, but the relationship hasn't been damaged because you haven't made an accusation.

# 4

# How to Unlock
# New Information

Several years ago, my wife and I decided to transfer our son from one school to another. He was a fifth grader in a parochial school, and at the end of the year we transferred him to a school with more resources to challenge him. Transferring him to the new school in sixth grade enabled him to interact with an entirely new class of students. We selected an all-boys school that has a lower, middle, and high school. It was our hope that the transition would go well in middle school and sustain itself into high school so that he would not have to change schools again. I would like to share with you an experience that my son had the first month of school that relates to the topic of this chapter.

I remember vividly coming home after conducting a seminar at the end of September. It was early evening. When I saw my son, I remembered that he had had his first test at the new school, and I wanted to find out how he did. The subject was history, one that he excelled at in his other school. When I asked him to explain to me how the test went, his response was, "It was stupid." Over the years, my wife and I have learned how to interpret his language and comments. What he was actually saying was, "The test was hard!" I asked him to share with me what was on the test. He said the first part was okay, multiple choice questions, but the second part was ridiculous. (This was another way for him to say that it was really difficult.) I asked him what made it hard, and he said it was the essay questions. I asked him if he could recall one of the questions and share it with me. The last question on his sixth-grade history test was: If Custer were to fight Napoleon, how would the two go about the conflict?

I will admit that I stood in front of him trying to conceal my reaction. Personally, I had no idea what the answer was. I was even thinking to myself, "You are right, son, that question is ridiculous." A second or two later, after I composed myself, I said to him, "What the school is trying to teach you is critical thinking." That is what this book and chapter introduces. Critical thinking is the key to your sales success.

## Critical Thinking

Critical thinking gets customers out of their box. Allow me to explain the importance of critical thinking to creating a sustainable sales relationship. During my graduate work in training and development, I had the good fortune of taking a psychology class taught by a professor named Dr. Paul Hilt. Little did I realize how his class would affect me in years to come. As I moved through the semester, I was captivated by the way people learn. The topic of left- and right-brain dominance was introduced through something called the Herrmann brain dominance inventory test. This test identified how people incorporate information. In a sense, it is another tool that can be used to determine how people receive information. If you are familiar with personality types, this topic would fall into this category of processing information.

Toward the middle of the semester, Professor Hilt asked me for a favor. He wanted to know if I would be willing to assist him in reviewing more than 20 years of research relating to the way people communicate. At first I was somewhat reluctant. It sounded like a lot of work, and I really didn't have the time. Then I realized that he had been very helpful to me and very insightful when it came to the material he presented in class, and now he needed my help. So I signed on to help. Most of the material I reviewed talked about open and closed questions.

# Open-Probe and Closed-Probe Questions

Most people who are reading this book or who are familiar with consultative selling have probably been introduced to the concept of open- and closed-probe questions. Probing is just another way of saying questioning, and the idea behind it involves gathering information and discovering a customer's needs.

There are two kinds of probing questions: open probes and closed probes. Closed probes limit the range of a customer's responses to yes or no. Also, there is a limited range of answers, based on the alternatives supplied. A closed-probe question is likely to begin with words such as: *do, is, are, have, has, did,* or *which.* They might include questions such as:

- Did your department make its goal?
- Are you looking for a way to eliminate that problem?
- Do you find that a problem?

- Did you receive any complaints?
- Which of these problems most affected your operation?

The answers you can expect from a closed-probe question are somewhat limited—a short answer, such as yes or no, or a validation of a topic. For example if you ask the question, "Do your patients listen to what you say?" the doctor would probably respond with an answer such as, "Most of the time," "I think so," or, "Not as much as I would like."

There is a good chance that these kinds of responses, which are typical of what you get when you ask a closed-probe question, will be short and to the point. They are not apt to move you closer to your goal of starting a meaningful conversation. These questions do, however, confirm and validate information.

On the other hand, an open-probe question encourages a lengthier reply. Open-probe questions are likely to begin with words like: *who, when, where, why, tell me, how,* and *what.* Some examples include:

- What are your goals for this year?
- In what areas are you looking to improve?
- Tell me about your application?
- Who is involved in the selection process and what is their role?
- When did you begin to notice the problem and what happened after that?
- How has the system been working?

As you can see, these questions are likely to lead to longer responses. Probing questions are the cornerstone of the selling process; unfortunately, these questions will not help you advance your existing relationship. Many of them have been answered before and generate a recitation response.

# Do Open Probes
# Differentiate You?

Let's go back to your mission as a salesperson. Your goal is to differentiate and brand yourself, gather key information, and move your existing relationships forward. Chances are that the customer views what you are selling as somewhat similar to what the competition is providing. There are probably few products or services offered in today's market that are remarkably different from the competition and that offer significant price differences or better service. As a matter of fact, the customer probably assumes that both you and the people you compete against will provide relatively the same thing. Therefore, you are being viewed as the same as the competition, almost like a commodity. Of course you want to establish a strong business relationship, separate yourself, stand out, and become a significant partner in the customer's business. To make that occur, you need to ask better questions.

We have been told that business surveys suggest that the "business" relationship between salesperson and customer is often the most important factor in the sales process. As a matter of fact, a number of years ago, the New York Sales and Marketing Club conducted a survey to determine what influences a person in business to buy a product or service. The top three answers were: relationship, success, and best. Out of the three, relationship was the most influential. According to the NYSMC, 38 percent of the time a customer will select a product or service because of the relationship with the salesperson. Success received the second highest total with 20 percent. Best was third at 18 percent. Almost by a two to one margin relationships influenced decisions according to this survey. But will asking the classic open- and closed-ended questions get you to where you need to be? I suggest that the open- and closed-probes are only a part of what it takes to evolve and sustain a business relationship. So what gets you there? Let's go look at research I was conducting during my graduate work.

## Asking the Right Kinds of Questions

During my analysis of 20 years of research on the way people communicate, I came across several interesting articles and studies that made me think a little differently about questions, how they are presented, and the way salespeople ask them to build and develop relationships. Some of the research looked at the way questions were posed in the classroom. For example, when a question is posed to a class and a student responds with a wrong answer, the class might perceive the student as being less smart than the rest of the class, and the student may not respond in the future. Do you see how that could happen in a sales call? How do you ask your question? What is your tone and inference? The way you ask questions will factor into the way the customer receives and responds to them.

A study conducted a number of years ago looked into the way teachers posed questions to their students. The study was commissioned to discover why most children give limited responses when they are asked a question. The results could also apply to dealing with our children or speaking with our spouses or significant others. For example: I am blessed with three children. If you are a parent, aunt, or uncle reading this book, I am sure that you have probably experienced the following. And even if you haven't, you will appreciate the story. Our family lifestyle tends to be somewhat hectic because our children are involved in many different activities. These activities range from sporting events and practices to rehearsals, shows, and recitals. Because of all these commitments, we don't sit down as a family at the dinner table as often as we'd like. This time, we were all gathered at the dinner table, and I turned to my oldest daughter and asked, "How was your day?" She replied, "It was fine." I then asked her, "What did you do in school today?" If you have children in school, you probably know that the number one answer to this question is "nothing." So, somewhat frustrated with my daughter's answer, I turned to my son. At times my son can talk up a storm. So, I asked him, "What did you do today in school?" He looked at me with somewhat of a puzzled expression and said, "I can't remember." "Nothing," and, "I can't remember." I sat there shaking my head and pondering the answers I received from my children. Now let's return to the world of selling and the studies that I read.

These studies focused on the fact that too many recital questions were being asked in the classroom. A recital question is a question that is asked of individuals that gets them to recite what they already know. Educator Meredith Gall suggested that recital questions get someone to recall information that requires little-to-no thinking. As a matter of fact, there is a high probability that a recital question has been asked and answered in some form in prior conversations. So when a customer answers a recital question, she recites something she already knows and probably has already been asked before in previous conversations. Let us think about this for a moment. Allow us to simmer on this: A recital question gets the customers to recite what they already know.

Think of all of the questions that you asked prior to reading this book. Do your questions fall under the category of recital? If so, is it possible that you might be boring your customers, because you are forcing them to go over the same ground they have been going over with everyone else? Let's take this thought a little further. How many salespeople do you think your customer sees in a day? One sales representative? Two salespeople? Could your customer see as many as ten salespeople per day? For argument's sake, why don't we settle on five salespeople a day? That is 25 a week, 100 per month, and more than 1,000 sales calls and conversations per year. Is it possible that your customer has heard the same question, day in and day out, year in and year out? The customer hears the same question hundreds of times and gives the same answer. Just like our children, they get bored answering the same old questions. I am guessing that you get the picture.

Chris Kane, a training manager for a large medical device company, agrees with this. He states:

> Our medical device teams had been wrestling with the challenge of how to approach a customer with whom they've had a long-standing relationship and answer the question "What's new?" or some generic variation. We have a very tenured sales team, many who have been in the same business and geography for a long time. With these customers, they have established a baseline relationship that ranges from the excellent (advocate) to the casual (occasional user) to those who support our competitors. They are likely on a very friendly basis with these customers and have access to them but are at a plateau situation with regards to business. During the times when there are no new products to offer, it has been a challenge to elevate the conversation to another level. The concept of recital versus dialogue questions has provided the platform from which this discussion could advance. Our sales associates are more confident that

they now have a tool with which to engage our customers in a more substantial dialogue. They view this as a way to open the door (again) and to relate on the customer's level and discuss *their needs* from *their* perspective.

## So What Makes a Better Question?

The study of classroom questioning suggested changing from a recital question to a dialogue question. Dialogue questions stimulate a complex thinking process involving a longer exchange that solicits opinion and thought, not just a correct answer. When calling on customers, you want to engage them in dialogue. Your goal is to get them talking at least 70 percent of the time. Most important, when you ask a dialogue question, you create the possibility of change. And change leads to new thinking. This is key: Change leads to new thinking from the customer. Your goal is to craft a question that gets the customer to stop, reflect, and respond with a new answer.

At the beginning of this book, you were introduced to the term *schema* and the importance of getting customers out of their "boxes." At the outset of a relationship, there is a need to gather information. You need to build your intelligence on customers and learn what is occurring at their company. This is accomplished by asking open- and closed-probe questions. During this process, you run the risk of boring and tiring out your customers as you get them to parrot back to you the same information everyone else is getting. This brings up another problem. You are getting, for the most part, the same information that everyone else is getting. If this is true, you are molding your solutions around the identical pieces of information that everyone you are competing with also possesses. So what distinguishes you from someone else? Your price? I hope not, because that is a slippery slope that no one wants to go down. Because once that is started, you can't stop the slide.

## The Light Bulb Is Going On

I am guessing the light bulb is going on, and it probably is glowing brightly about now. Some of you may be thinking, "Am I lucky to have gotten this far with some of my customers?" As a review, the questions that you have been asking have enabled you to move some of your relationships to the highest level. Your questions have worked. You got the customer to reveal more information to you than to your competition. However, it is becoming clear why a number of other business relationships are stalling out and idling in neutral. Could it be the questions that you are asking? According to sales director Nick Martino, this is exactly why relationships stall out. Martino states that:

> From the perspective of us selling to our customers, we take a slightly different approach. First we do what is called "80/20" our accounts. This is the simplified process of using the Pareto Principle to differentiate between accounts and use a decision-making tool to determine the value proposition to our business and also what value proposition we can bring to the account. If there is a marriage, the account is focused on for development. The fundamental driving force is to ascertain how we can mutually benefit from each other and whether or not there is merit in pursuing the account. I

take this practice to heart. Each manager and salesperson under my direction needs to determine the needs (mid and long term) for both parties—us and the prospective customer—it is our job to deliver value to one of these needs each time we visit. This keeps the relationship fresh as the "story" we are telling always has value. It is the responsibility of the manager and his sales team to determine what they share, and why—but *they must be telling something new on each visit!* A good example is Nike Corporation—they maintain a vigil internally that says, "if you can give us a story line about a new product, new process or innovative environmental contribution, we can package it and sell it." This is the basis on which our sales team now focuses to keep the relationship alive with our primary accounts.

## Keeping It Alive

Success isn't certain, even when salespeople encourage customers to talk. Why? Because just having a regular conversation won't accomplish your objective of getting the customer "out of the box."

The fact is that there is a substantial difference between just making conversation, like you might at a cocktail party, and making *meaningful* in-depth discussion. By meaningful discussion, I mean those that create *meaningful* dialogue, provide you with *meaningful* information, and ultimately set you apart from the salespeople who come in, make idle chatter, and dominate the call.

So how do you involve someone in a meaningful discussion? Think about it for a minute. Do you have any ideas? The easiest way to involve people in a conversation is to ask them a question. But what kind of a question do you need to ask to evoke the type of response that's meaningful?

Questions elicit responses. They provide you with the information that you need to move the sales cycle along. They enable a conversation, and they help initiate a relationship. Typically when I make these points in my seminars, someone will say, "I ask questions all the time." And I respond, "Yes, most salespeople ask questions." But, more often than not, salespeople don't ask enough questions or, more significantly, the right kind of questions.

To illustrate my point, I'd like you to take a couple of minutes to write the questions that you often ask customers on the telephone or during a sales call to discover their needs. See if you can come up with your ten *best* questions.

1. _____

2. _____

3. _____

4. _____

5. _____

6. _____

7. _____

8. _____

9. _____

10. _____

Usually when I do this exercise with a group of salespeople, most participants think it is going to be a snap. They start off with a great deal of confidence, but a few minutes into the exercise some of them start to squirm. It seems that it is much harder than you think to come up with 10 good questions.

If you couldn't come up with 10 questions, don't worry. Very few people do. In fact, the average at one of my seminars is somewhere between 6 and 7 questions. In a study I conducted, 87 percent of the salespeople that participated in our programs said that they knew the importance of asking questions. But only 27 percent, slightly more than a quarter, were then able to demonstrate the ability to ask a well-thought-out question that would stimulate dialogue.

It became clear to me quite early on that most salespeople need to improve their ability to ask questions that generate dialogue. What do I mean by that? If a salesperson or sales representative is asking a customer questions, the typical ones could be:

1. What are your challenges?
2. How many manufacturing facilities do you have?
3. Where are they located?
4. If you could change one thing, what would it be?
5. What keeps you up at night?
6. Who are your current vendors?
7. What is your budget?

There is nothing wrong with these recitation-provoking types of questions. Very often they elicit baseline information that you need in order to develop a meaningful solution for the customer, and they are a necessary ingredient of every sales call. But customers providing a recitation response are simply giving you information they already know. There's no thought involved and no real opportunity to move in new directions. As a matter of fact, you might be boring customers and prompting them to wonder when the conversation will be over.

Beyond that, recitation responses are very often available from sources other than your customer. If I were a customer, I'd have serious reservations about a potential vendor who took up much of my time asking me how many plants my company has, where they are, how many patients I might see in a day, how many audits I conduct in a year, or who my current suppliers are. So do a little homework and see if you can answer these questions yourself. Once you have gathered that information, it would be acceptable to validate what you have learned with the customer.

Moreover, asking those kinds of questions is the same as opening the conversation by marveling at the stuffed swordfish I have mounted behind my desk. Everyone who comes in asks me the same thing, "Did you catch that fish?"

## Dialogue Questions

Dialogue probing questions are designed to elicit thought. They aren't designed simply to get an answer. Their intent is to make the customer think differently and to open up new avenues for discussion. They are crafted in a way to get the customer "out of the box." The potential benefits of a dialogue question are numerous. They will help you achieve several of your goals, such as gaining more information, differentiating yourself from the competition, and moving the customer's thought process forward.

One of the most obvious benefits is that customers will look at you differently. I cannot tell you how many times students have told me after they finish my class that the customer will say, "You know, no one has ever asked me that before," or, "That was a really great question." When a customer says that, you are making progress in differentiating yourself from the pack. Customers will look at you differently from the way they look at the "how many manufacturing plants do you have" salespeople who try to access their domain day in and month out. You will have initiated the process of creating a meaningful difference. And chances are you will have earned some respect as well as taken the first important step toward building a long-term business relationship.

## The Status Quo Might Be Good— for the Customer

It is important to realize that the customer has granted you permission to speak with her. She has brought a certain set of expectations to the sales call and is aware you are there to sell something. And you, the salesperson, should realize that the customer is trying to stay the same and maintain the status quo. This is discussed in Chapter 2 and relates to a customer's schema. If the information doesn't fit in with customers' past experiences, they will start to assess blame. Unless a problem occurs, causing the customer to realize the need for change (vendor, product/ service) you are tasked with getting the customer "out of the box." From the customers' point of view, their mission is, "If it ain't broke, don't fix it." In a sense, there are two conflicting messages. You, the salesperson, are trying to get the customer to change, and the customer is trying to resist change. If this is so, there is a need to create a compelling case for the customer to do something differently because if the customer agrees to do something differently, it will take time, require additional resources, and create focus on him, his department, and his operation.

# Your Job Description

If you think about your role as a sales professional, it is quite clear: you are hired to change the way people think. If they are not selecting your product or service, your challenge is to get them to do so. If they are using your product or service, your challenge is to get them to use it more. Therefore, you are hired to create change. The best way to create change is by creating a dialogue.

By literally forcing the customer to think and perhaps look at something from a different perspective, you raise the possibility of change. You will know that you have a shot at success if the customer says, "You know I never looked at it that way."

Finally, dialogue creates a sense of intimacy and trust. And once you accomplish that, you've bridged the gap from an anonymous salesperson to a salesperson with an understanding of what needs to get done. And as I've discussed previously, surveys of buyers indicate that their relationship with the salesperson is one of the key factors in the buy/don't buy decision-making process.

Now that you understand the importance of creating an atmosphere of dialogue, we'll discuss the art of asking questions and how to build those skills, as well as the different types of questions and when to ask them. Mastering these skills is at the very heart of the process that will transform you from just a good salesperson to a super salesperson.

# 5

# Getting More from Your Questions

Over the years I have studied professionals involved in interviewing individuals. I watch them ask questions and hear how people respond. It has given me a pathway to understanding how to ask better questions. Asking better questions is one of the critical elements for your success.

## Why Do We Need Better Questions?

If you are reading this book, there is a good possibility that you have a number of established relationships in business. Because the relationships are established, a different tone is set at the beginning of your call or conversation. There tends to be a lighter, if not friendlier, atmosphere to the sales call. Most of the time, the beginning of the call starts with the nice chitchat stuff. It is the idle banter that allows you to get caught up with the other person. The conversation could center on something involving your customers' personal life, their interests (sports, outdoors, hobbies, etc.) or family. After a couple of minutes go by, the first awkward moment that occurs in every established relationship happens, the moment when the customer finally says, "So what's up with your company?" or "What's new?" or "I'm a little tight on time. What do you have for me today?" At that moment, there is a need for you to ask a question. There is a need for you to try to elevate the discussion into dialogue. There is a need for you to avoid slipping back into the recital abyss and being just like everyone else. If a good question is not asked at this moment, the customer will probably politely listen and find a way to manage you out of the office or work space.

## Formulating the Right Questions

Once I realized the need to ask dialogue questions that generate new information, I set out to build a template on how to make this happen. During the process, I came across several different styles before I crafted the information in this chapter. During the maturation process of crafting a better question, I watched several renowned individuals apply their craft. One person that comes to mind quickly is Barbara Walters. There was something about the way she asked questions that got people to open up and share intimate information with a video camera and lights running in the background. Whether you are a fan of Barbara Walters or not, I am guessing that there is a good possibility you have seen at least one of her interviews. For the most part, she interviews celebrities or people in the news. They can range from entertainers to politicians to heroes to athletes. Inevitably, the person she is questioning will say, "Barbara, I have never said this before." That is what you are after, to get the customer to share new information that others have not yet heard. If you are a fan of Barbara Walters, you also know that many of the people she interviews cry. Some of you reading this book might be thinking, can you teach me how to get that difficult customer to break down in tears? I am not sure I can make that happen, but I think I can share with you a way to get the customer to open up and reveal new and different information.

Allow me to demonstrate what I am talking about. A number of years ago, during the Clinton administration, we were introduced to a person by the name of George Stephanopoulos. At the time, he was a member of Clinton's staff. For nearly two terms of office, Stephanopoulos would field questions from the media about Clinton's policies, ideas, and behavior. I watched him as much as possible because I felt that he was extremely skilled at answering difficult questions. It seemed like there was nothing the media could throw at him to trip him up. Clearly he was a talent when it came to managing difficult situations. Prior to his departure from the Clinton administration, I recall an interview that captured my attention. When Clinton ran for his second term, it was fairly obvious on election night that he would have a landslide victory. Before it was made final and Senator Bob Dole delivered his concession speech, Maria Shriver approached Stephanopoulos on the White House lawn. It was around 8 p.m. eastern standard time. It was live television. Maria Shriver asked him, "George, on a personal note, how does tonight compare to four years ago?" Cameras rolling, lights on, the master at fielding the media's questions stood speechless for several seconds. Finally, he answered the question. Eureka! That was it. The ultimate master at deflecting questions with a quick response was stumped. He couldn't just rapid-fire answer the question. He had to think about it before he answered. That is what we are going to do. Create questions that make customers think about their answers, ponder their choices, and provide a new and different response. At that moment, I realized what dialogue is all about. It's about getting people to reveal new information, while all along they have been giving lip service and providing the same old answers to those who have been asking the same questions when soliciting information.

## Creating Dialogue

That interview set me on a path to develop a template that gets people to share more information. Let's start out with something simple and mundane. Most of us have talked to some individual in the last several months who has taken a vacation or went on a trip. When we see or call the person after the trip, we tend to ask some questions about the experience. The first question is normally, "How was your trip?" The most common response is, "Great, too short." Hmm. The follow-up question could be, "What did you do?" I think you are getting the idea. We ask the same questions most of the time. And we get the same answers most of the time. As a matter of fact, if you were to go back to the list of the 10 most common questions that you ask your customer, I would be willing to say that at least half of your questions start with *how* and *what*. You are asking how and what, your competition is asking how and what, so guess what: Your customer is giving you and everyone else exactly the same answer. You are getting the same information everyone else is. Therefore, your solution, product, or service appears to be the same. Your pricing is probably compatible and competitive. So why should the customer change if there is no real perceived benefit in going through all the effort and exposure to do something different?

## Make Your Questions Better

Start watching television. I am not suggesting that you become a fan of reality television. I am suggesting that, every once in a while, you catch a program that asks a lot of questions. Some of the programming that is on Sunday mornings requires questions. A presidential press conference requires questions. An interview with an athlete, coach, or manager requires questions. Listen to how the questions are formulated and the way people respond. Does it seem that the answers are somewhat contrived? Are the questions meaningful, redundant, pertinent, or safe to answer? I am asking you to become your own judge. See whether you can pick up a pattern or style that you like best. Also, watch people in the media to help you determine what you do and don't like. Are some interviewers too abrupt? Are they too hard on the people they talk to? Are the questions too simple or inappropriate? Does it seem that the interviewers are trying to trap the people they're talking to instead of creating a safe environment?

Recently, in a seminar I conducted on the East Coast with a group of highly seasoned sales professionals, I was stopped by a participant about an hour into the session. I had just run the group through the process of determining whether their questions were just a recital or were a real dialogue. One individual raised his hand. When I called on him to find out what he wanted, he said to me and the entire group, "Not only are my questions a recital, but I am creating a debate with my customer." He went on to say, "If I create a debate with my customer, I will lose the debate and most certainly will lose the customer's trust and access." Some interviewers create a debate. If you create a debate, there is a good chance you will lose the opportunity of moving the relationship forward.

Questions need to be meaningful, targeted, and focused on each particular customer. If you have an established relationship with certain customers, meaning you have been in contact with them for quite some time, there is a good chance that your questions are running out of steam. If you look back and determine that most of your questions starting with who, what, when, where, and why have already been answered, so where do you go next? In a sense, your original questions have already been answered and have no more usefulness

Bonnie Luizza, a trainer for a Fortune 100 company, shared with me that the questioning skills content presented in this book are real-world, relevant, and practical. By the end of the workshop, her sales representatives are simply amazed at how they are able to significantly improve the quality of their questions. She goes on to say that, "the greatest learning occurs when representatives realize how many of their questions (which they originally thought were quality questions) are actually recital questions that don't stimulate critical thinking and don't enhance the discussion." After completing the session on questioning skills, one sales professional remarked how much more in-depth her dialogue was with her customers as a result of the dialogue questioning techniques learned in class and presented in this book.

## Make It about Them

Before you recraft your questions with the advice you are about to receive, let's first focus your attention on who benefits from the answers to your questions. Earlier, you were introduced to the concept of recital versus dialogue questions. As you recall, the recital question is a question that gets customers to recite

what they already know. A minimum of "out of the box" thinking occurs. Let's reassess your questions. Go back to the list of
10 questions you wrote earlier. We found that most of them
(about 80 percent) are recital questions. But what percentage of
your questions are meaningful? Reassess your questions to determine whether they are sales- or customer-focused.

## Sales- or Customer-Focused Questions

Jeff Taylor is the senior director of sales training for a Fortune 500
company in the pharmaceutical industry. Jeff shared that "over
the last decade my industry has seen increasing pressure on doctors to see more and more patients. This in turn has limited the
doctors' time to interact with the representative." Taylor goes on
to say that his company's sales managers and field sales teams
report that their two biggest challenges are first getting acccss to
their customers and second engaging them for a sufficient amount
of time to fully communicate the benefits of their products.

Taylor stated that "industry market research data provides
insight into this problem as well as suggesting a possible solution. The most significant finding was the overriding theme,
which suggests that too many sales professionals approach a sales
call from their own perspective and the perspective of their product, not from the customer's perspective." The research referred
to this as a product-focused rather than a customer-focused
approach. Taylor has also noticed that when this occurs in the
field, it is not a good situation if the customer is looking for "a
sincere interest and understanding of the problems in his or her
practice and the salesperson is focused on their story."

During a several-year period, members of Taylor's department realized this gap and made adjustments to correct the problem. Using the skills presented in this book, they put their sales

professionals on the correct path to being more customer-focused by asking engaging and thought-provoking questions. The results after 90 days indicated that access had increased, total time with the customer improved during each call, and most importantly the dialogue with the customer was focused on the customer. These changes demonstrated greater impact for more than 75 percent of sales calls.

## Improve Impact

A sales-focused question has three elements that can raise a red flag. These are (1) Do you mention your product or service in your question? For example, "Do you like your XYZ product?" (2) Do you ask a question that creates a product-to-product or service-to-service comparison? An example of this type of question would be, "Can you tell me how our service stacks up against what you are already using?" Another version of this question would involve your mentioning the product or service the customer is currently using. For example, "Are you satisfied with your current product or service? What is it that you like or dislike about your current product or service?" For customers to answer these types of questions, either they have to support their selection, which makes it more difficult for you to sell, or they have to indicate that their product or service selections in the past have been poor choices. There is a good possibility that customers will not willingly say that they have made a mistake. Even if you ask the customer the "magic-wand" question, which is, "If you were to have a magic wand, what would the perfect product or service look like?" Once again, this is suggesting that what they are doing now is somewhat flawed. The art of questioning is about creating an atmosphere of complete disclosure and trust. At times, with an established relationship, these kinds of questions will fail you in your ability to move the existing relationship forward. (3) When the customer answers the questions, which person benefits from the response—you or the customer? An example of this question would be, "What seems to be your biggest challenge to improve production? What happens in your department that keeps you up at night?" Once again, these are not bad questions. They are open-ended, but the customer does not gain additional insight or value from answering them. The answers benefit only the salesperson. Only when the questions start to benefit the customer, will you break through and sell at another level. Dialogue questions are *all* about the customer. And if it becomes all about the customer, it will become all about moving your market share and increasing sales. Make it about customers, not about you. Let me also suggest that many of your sales-focused questions have worked. These questions have gotten some relationships to the highest levels; however, some of your relationships have reached a peak and are going sideways.

## Breaking It Down

Many of your questions could be just a recital. Many of those questions are probably sales-focused. Therefore, a good number of your questions may be falling short when it comes to advancing relationships. It appears that there may be a need for you to change the way you ask questions in order for you to align with the concept of creating dialogue and customer-focused questions.

# Crafting a Dialogue Question

There are several things to consider when crafting a dialogue question. The first is that your customer will not be expecting a dialogue probing question. The customer will be expecting the types of questions that you listed early in your most commonly asked questions worksheet. These are the questions that are easy for customers to answer. These are the questions they are familiar with and readily have an answer for because they have heard these questions over and over again. When you ask your customer a dialogue question, you are doing something new. And because we are going to be trying something different, there is a need to get the customer ready for the question. There is a need to transition from the normal banter of conversation that occurs at the beginning of a sales call or conversation to the dialogue question.

The opportunity for dialogue really begins when the existing or prospective customer asks, "What do you have for me today?" When this occurs, there is a need to transition to the dialogue question. This means that you need to get your customers prepared for the question. Since it is going to be a different type of question, they need to be ready for it. An analogy I can provide is when I was taking an art class in college. I remember the professor saying, "You need to prepare the canvas before the paint." I remember wondering, why can't I just paint? At the first break, I approached the professor and asked him that question—why can't I just paint? He responded by saying, "Because it won't stick." He went on to explain that the canvas needed to be "sized" so the paint would be absorbed. Sizing is putting on a coat prior to the paint to close all the pores in the canvas. His explanation seemed to make sense. The same analogy can be used when painting a new piece of wood or drywall. If you start trying to paint with the finish coat, without putting on a primer, the paint will be absorbed and will evaporate into the drywall or wood. However, if you first add a primer to seal the open pours of the wood or drywall, the material (wood or drywall) will be prepared for the finish coat. The same is true with your customer. I guess you can view customers as drywall. So prep them first.

# Process for Dialoguing

Much like the canvas, we need to get the customer ready for a better question. First, we need to provide a transition.

## *Transition*

A transition can be simple or involved. When the customer says to you, "What do you have for me today?" you can transition with something as simple as, "I would like to ask you a couple of quick questions," or something a bit more elaborate like, "I would like to run a couple of questions by you and hear how your answers compare to several others in your department, industry, company, etc." The first is short and sweet. The second is more comprehensive. The second could excite customers and get them to listen more intently because they don't want to give a bad answer or appear less aware than other colleagues. Either way, the transition is required to move customers to a position where they can accept the dialogue question. There is one caveat which needs to be considered that applies to when you are asking questions of your "friend" customer. The "friend" customer is someone who knows you pretty well. He or she can sense when you are trying something different. You want to avoid the friend saying, "What happened to you? Did you just attend a sales seminar or read a book or something?" To avoid this from happening or to minimize how often it happens, the following transition is suggested: "Mr. or Ms. Customer, I have a question for you, and it is a little different. I would really like to hear how you respond to it." Setting up your dialogue question in this manner builds in a little wiggle room. It is saying to the customer, here comes something different. Please listen to the question and give me an honest answer. At times the honest answer could be a response to the question. At other times, the honest answer may be a recommendation on how to recraft the question. Either way, it is a win for you because you are attempting to move the customer out of his or her box.

Other transition examples are:

I would like to get your opinion on . . .
I would like to run something by you (this is one of my favorites).
I have a quick question for you.
I hope you could share with me your opinion or experience about a situation, case, event, and so forth.
Could I get your thoughts on a particular issue?

These are examples of just a few transitions. There are certainly many more. As people develop into advanced sales professionals, I have learned that the use of transitions assists in the continuity of a sales call and keeps things running smoothly. Most of us realize that we need to ask questions, listen, and present solutions and gain commitment. However, very little time is spent on transitions. To avoid the lulls in the conversation and seamlessly move from one topic to another, there is a need to know how to transition.

Many years ago when I first started learning how to sell, I attended as many sales seminars as I could. I went to one at least once a month. I read a number of books and listened to a lot of tapes. It goes back to what I talked about at the beginning of this book on "going pro." In any event, I remember attending a sales seminar that was led by a known sales trainer. The topic was closing. I remember one of his techniques that I didn't like. The closing technique was about guiding people to the answer you wanted them to provide. The example that was given was about choosing a color. The color choices were black and white. The scenario was that you would present a customer with a color choice (black or white). For example, let's say you wanted the customer to pick white. You tell the customer that there are two colors—black and white—and say, "Pick one." The first customer would pick white. You were then instructed to say, "Correct," and go on to ask another question. The next customer was given the same choice; however, the second customer picked black. Black was not the choice you wanted him or her to make. However, the seminar taught you to say, "So that leaves us with white." My first reaction was, wow, that is manipulative. Looking back, I still feel that technique is manipulative; however, it was all about transitioning. Years later, I realized that it was about transitioning without missing a beat. I didn't like the methods for closing the sale; however, it was a good example of how to transition.

Transitioning is a little identified art. Especially with established relationships, it is important to know how to transition, how to steer the conversation in the most productive way. Come up with some transitions that you like and feel comfortable with. One of my favorites is, "I would like to run something by you . . ." Or "That being said, let me ask you this . . ." These are everyday phrases that come off naturally. If you know how to transition as well as how to apply a conversational tone to your questions and presentations, you will move along with a minimum number of bumps. Having a good grasp on transitions and conversational language is like taking a boat out on a lake that looks like glass—not a ripple. It is easy to drive and to drive fast. Without transitions, you will have to navigate some high waves, the trip will be a little bumpy, and it will take longer. Now that the customer is ready for a different question, let's ask it.

## Starting the Dialogue Question

The second step in creating a better question is to learn how to start it. Most of our everyday questions start with words like who, what, when, why, and how. If you were to take a look at many of the questions that you ask in your everyday professional and personal life, most of them will start with one of the above-mentioned words. And therein lies the problem. Most of your and everyone else's questions are about the same. What does the normal conversation sound like when you come home at night after a short or long day at work? What tends to be the first thing you ask when you arrive home and get settled? The first question to your roommate, spouse, family member, or significant other is likely, "How was your day?" And the most common response to that question is, "Fine." The follow-up question the other person asks is, "How was yours?" The response you will probably give is, "Not bad." The finale is, "Okay, so what's for dinner?" This may or may not reflect your conversation when you come home at night, but I think you get the picture. We can all fall into ruts. We fall into ruts when we ask our customers questions. For those of you who call on the customer on a repeated basis, you can fall into more of a rut. For example, did you ever pull up to the customer's location and sit in your car thinking, "What am I going to do today? What in the world am I going to ask? I have asked everything up to this point."

How do we get out of the rut? Ask your questions differently by starting them differently. Search for words or phrases that will get the customer to think differently. That's worth repeating: Get your customer to think differently. This one element alone will not get your customers out of their box, but it is a start. Instead of using overused words like who, what, when, where, and why, try something different. Use words like describe, explore, and explain. Let's go back to the example about coming home at night. Instead of saying, "How was your day?" (which tends to generate a limited response), rephrase the question by asking, "Describe for me what took place in your day." You can see that this approach forces the person to give more thought to a response and avoids the rapid-fire answer, "Fine."

By starting your question differently, you open up the other person. To open up the customer, you can also try using phrases. Phrases are my personal favorite: for example, "Can you please tell me a little bit about . . ." When you select the types of words you will use to open up your questions, make sure that they fit your style and the styles of the people you are talking to. At first, students in my class push back when they hear me suggest the use of words like describe or explain. But, as I point out to the class, such words encourage more of an in-depth response. Some students will say that is not how they talk. Agreed. You need to rephrase these questions in your own voice. For over 29 years, a business colleague, friend, and eventual vice president of my company, Jim McAlea, enjoyed starting his questions with, "Could you share with me?" That was his style. He liked asking questions that way. He got results because it was his style. I remember that most times when he would come back to our office after making sales calls; our staff almost in unison would ask, "Did you get the customer to share with you today?" He smiled and nodded.

When creating a dialogue question, you need to find your own voice. Determine what works for you. Are you comfortable starting the question with words like describe, explain, or explore? Or is it more natural for you to start the question with a phrase that you are particularly comfortable with, one that will work for you? Following are examples of phrases you can use to start a dialogue:

Could you please share with me . . .
Would you tell me a little bit about . . .
Please walk me through . . .
I would like to get your opinion on . . .
Please tell me about . . .

These are only some of the many different phrases you can use to start a dialogue. The customer's comfort level is equally as important as yours. For the most part, there are four different personality styles an individual customer can have. The most commonly identified words used to describe these four styles are: controlling, amiable, expressive, and analytical. Other terms sometimes encountered include: steady, compliant, influencing, dominant, type A, or conscientious. More detailed classifications of personality or communication styles can be separated into sub-groups within each quad, with initials as identifiers, but our discussion will focus on the four basic categories: controlling, amiable, expressive, and analytical.

Let's take, for example, the controlling, or driver, personality. This is the type A controller, who likes things (for the most part) short and sweet. If you were to start your question to a controller-type customer with, "Could you please walk me through your thoughts . . .?" that customer's brain might explode. Such an approach would take too much effort and time for the controller to answer such a question. It would be better to simply start the question with, "Please tell me about . . ."—an approach that better aligns with the controller's makeup.

Table 5.1 provides some helpful hints about how to start questions or requests based on each customer's personality style.

| Customer Personality Type | Appropriate Approach for Questioning Customer |
|---|---|
| Analytical | Describe for me your thoughts ... |
| Controlling | Please tell me about ... |
| Amiable | Could you please share with me ... |
| Expressive | I would like to get your opinion on ... |

**TABLE 5.1** Gearing Questions to a Customer's Personality Style

If for some reason, you are unfamiliar with the four basic personality styles or do not know how to identify someone's style, I would like to give you a quick rule of thumb that was taught to me a number of years ago. This is not as detailed and as accurate as the actual course, but the following can at least get you started in the correct direction: Ask your customer how he or she went about making a major decision like buying a car. Listen to the answer. If the customer tells you that he or she did a lot of research, checked out all of the automotive buyer's guides, reviewed all the safety ratings, and made comparisons, chances are you are dealing with an analytical personality. If the person says, "Well, many of my colleagues own the same car," this person is probably an amiable type. If the person says, "I think it makes me look great," this is certainly a person with an expressive personality. And finally, if the person says, "I gave it a test drive and bought it," this is a controlling personality.

Aligning your questions with the personality style of your customers assists in their acceptance and connection. More importantly, you the salesperson need to be comfortable in the delivery of the questions. During the development of our skills, we found out that approximately 80 percent of the time a customer will be comfortable answering your question, as long as you are comfortable asking it. Therefore, the more fluent and conversational you become with your questions, the better the delivery and the customer's acceptance. In a way, this is common sense; however, just like any skill, you need to work on it relentlessly until it becomes second nature. An example of practice makes perfect can be found in athletic competition. In games like golf and tennis, you will watch the athlete hit the ball effortlessly. Their swing and stroke are rhythmical. They are consistent. Much like a musician, they play their instruments and are immersed in the sound and feeling of the music. You can't reach this level of production and proficiency without a lot of practice. The same is true with the content of this book. A lot of practice is required to make the skills presented in the book second nature. This is another case about "going pro."

## Creating a Comparison— The Key to a Better Question

Part of the battle of asking a better question is getting a better start. Starting your questions with descriptive words or phrases encourages the customer to open up a little more. However, the key to a great question lies in something more important than a good start. The key to getting the customer—or anyone else as a matter of fact—out of the box is the need to create a comparison in your question. Creating a comparison forces the person you are speaking to, to stop, reflect, and respond. That is the key to getting new information. As a professional in selling you are trying to stop the customers from giving you the same old rote answer that they give to most other people.

Moving the customer from recital mode to dialogue mode is contingent upon creating a comparison. By creating a comparison, you are requesting that customers evaluate their current experience, knowledge base, basis, or position in relation to another piece of information.

## Completing the Dialogue Question

The concept of creating a comparison works when it comes to getting people to give you a different answer. Requesting a comparison gets people to sit back and ponder before they respond. Let's analyze a couple of everyday scenarios before we circle back to your world of professional selling. Earlier, I talked about the scenario that deals with a person taking a vacation. Normally you would ask the individual how the trip went. Based on the information in this chapter, you now may ask this person to describe the trip. To ensure a more comprehensive and possibly different answer, a comparison can be injected. For example, you are meeting a friend at a reception or party. The regular banter of meaningless discussion takes place. The topic of vacations is broached. Someone asks, "How was your recent vacation?" The person replies, "Great." At that moment, you can enter into the conversation by asking, "Tell me a little bit about this year's vacation compared to some of the others you took in prior years." Now that is a different question. Initially, you might have some reservations. But this different question works for several reasons. To make the question work, you need to adhere to what was just talked about in reference to the fluency of the delivery of the question. If the question is too choppy or disconnected, it will not work as well as it could have. If the question is delivered in a conversational and sincere tone, the person being asked the question will stop and consider the answer. The goal of creating a comparison is to stop the person from giving the rapid-fire answer. Think of yourself in this situation. If someone were to ask you that question, you would have to think about your most recent trip. You would then have to think back to your prior trips and determine your level of enjoyment. You would also have to evaluate each trip against the others and finally respond. You might say that this is too much work for a friend to respond to, but you might be surprised. Creating comparisons is a way of showing interest and engaging a person differently.

Consider the following: I am a sports fan. I happen to listen on occasion to sports talk radio. Every so often, there is a discussion about who was the best team of a decade, century, and so on. The radio host(s) will discuss who were the best teams in the National Football League (NFL), the National Basketball Association (NBA), or even the best college football or basketball teams of all time. These topics generate a lot of interest. The discussion is vibrant and at times passionate and heated. The bottom line is this: The radio hosts are creating comparisons. How does the best team in the nineties compare with those of prior decades? Or who was the best player of all time in the NBA? Was it some of the league's past greats or one of the current players? Style, athleticism, speed, and knowledge of the game are all compared. The answers are hypothetical, but they create a lot of thought and discussion. That is what you would like to happen in your conversations. Asking for this type of comparison not only stimulates a different, more thoughtful answer, but it also starts to distinguish you as someone who is a little more interesting than the next person.

# Types of Comparisons

There are many ways you can create comparisons. The most common comparisons can be based on time and trends. For example, "What has been your experience about (some) issue, and how does that compare to several years ago?" A time comparison gets the customers to consider their present situation and how it compares to the past several years. A good example of this could be someone who is in the financial field. If an investment advisor were to say to a client (individual investor), "Please tell me about your current investment strategy and compare it with your strategy over the past several years." You can see how this type of question can get the individual investor to open up. Chances are that the individual investors will lament about past performances and their original strategies and where they are currently positioned. Creating a comparison unleashes new information and at the same time allows you the salesperson to play the role of counselor, consultant, and advisor.

When you create a trend comparison with your customers, you are asking them to consider their current methods or approaches and to decide how these compare with what is taking place in the marketplace. If we were to look at the field of accounting, a question that might be asked to a Fortune 500 corporation's CFO (chief financial officer) could be, "Describe for me your approach to the new tax laws and how that compares to the approach of others in your industry or marketplace." A question like this allows the salesperson to understand not only the prospective client's opinion or position, but also how the client is aligned or misaligned with the marketplace. If we were to circle back to the world of investments, the issue of trends is extremely prevalent. Every day you can pick up a copy of the *Wall Street Journal* and read an article by an expert that suggests that one form of investing is better than another. In the same newspaper, you can often probably find an article stating the opposite. Getting the customer to create comparisons allows for a better discussion. In addition, a comparison is a safe conversation. Asking a client or customer to share his or her thoughts and experiences compared to something else is safe. A comparison does not back people into a corner. It gets them to share their view and compare it to a different view. It is safe and intellectually stimulating.

If we were to go back to my story about my son in middle school, his test question created a comparison. If Custer were to fight Napoleon, how would the two go about the conflict? That is a comparison. It gets the students to assess the theories and strategies of both leaders and compare them. It sets up a very thought-provoking answer. It requires the digestion of several pieces of information before the respondent can answer. That is what you want to happen in your sales calls and conversations. Get the customer to answer differently.

Comparisons can be based on time, trends, and comments from industry (thought) leaders, advantageous or adverse events, or changes in policies.

## Quality of the Comparison

By simply making a comparison, you elevate the chances of getting a different answer. The comparison in itself prompts a different answer. The quality of the comparison is what makes for a great question. Let's reexamine the idea of a customer-focused question versus a sales-focused question. If you were to ask the customer to compare your product to that of a competitor, initially the concept of creating a comparison is accomplished.

However, is the answer meaningful, safe, and productive? If you ask a customer to compare what he has selected in years past and compare that to what you are selling, is that a winning proposition? Probably not. You are actually asking the customer to tell you whether he made a good decision. If you ask a person who has purchased Ford trucks his entire life about how his thoughts about Ford compare to Chevrolet, what do you think he is going to say? He will defend his decision. If the customer defends his decision, you have dug yourself a deeper hole. You are not getting the customer out of the box. On the other hand, if the customer is polite, she will assess what you asked her and give you a politically correct response; something like this, "Chevy has some nice features." In the long run, the customer will tell you what you want to hear, so she can simply get rid of you. You leave the sales call thinking that you made progress and opened a couple of doors, but the reality is that you might have closed a few.

## Validating the Best Comparisons

Every so often, I will reach out to my client's customers to ensure the application and effectiveness of our concepts. I will hold focus groups several times a year and invite customers to attend. At these meetings we introduce new ideas (sales concepts) to get the feedback of the group. My firm learns a lot when these sessions are conducted. I share some of the findings of these meetings throughout this book.

During one of the meetings, I approached the group with this question: "Now that you have graduated from college, possibly obtained a master's, doctorate, or MBA, how do you keep yourself apprised of what is going on in your industry?" After a lengthy discussion, we came up with an answer. It appears that there are three most common ways that executives, doctors, lawyers, business owners (your customers) keep up with information. They are:

They read articles, journals, and reports.
They attend conferences and seminars and listen to webcasts and
     educational conference calls.
They talk among their peers.

The three best ways of creating a comparison is to focus on how your customer continues his education process. Our findings suggest the three most common ways of staying abreast of information are the above: reading, listening, and discussing among peers and colleagues. As a professional salesperson, you need to tap into that pool of information.

## Determine the Best Comparison

Just because my firm found out through our research what the most common ways a customer keeps up with information are doesn't mean that these are the ways your customer learns. Therefore, ask the customer how she continues to educate herself. You might remember earlier in this book that we talked about the open and closed probe. Those kinds of questions do not go away or become dormant. Those questions will always have an ongoing purpose and presence in a sales call. A closed probe as discussed can help you transition to a dialogue question. An open probe can keep the information process going. For this reason, during the next couple of sales calls or phone conversations you have with your customers, ask them this question. "Now that you have been out of school for a number of years and have completed your certification (this could be a doctor, lawyer, plumber, accountant, etc.), how do you keep up with getting information about your industry and the latest trends?" The answer to this question will give you the best form of comparison for your upcoming calls. Asking the open and closed probe to gather intelligence (you are like the CIA agent or detective getting information to put the pieces together) allows you to better plan and set up a more intellectually engaging conversation in the near future. So let's say your customer says, "I attend as many conferences as I can or the budget will allow me to register for." It appears that this customer likes to go and listen to others in her industry and experts surrounding her industry talk. If that is the case, your comparison (the end of the dialogue probing question) would be, "And how does this compare to what you have been hearing at some of the recent conferences you have attended?" This comparison connects, because this is how they keep up with information. On the other hand, what if the customer says, "I read a lot." Simply put, the end of the dialogue probe would be, "And how does this compare to some of the articles you have recently read?"

Connecting with your customers is paramount. Determining how they continue their education and knowledge allows you to better relate to them. And finally, if the customers are the type of people who like to hear about what others are doing (maybe an amiable personality style that makes decisions based on others), your comparison would be, "And compare that with some of the feedback you are receiving from your colleagues?"

Creating comparisons in this manner takes the customers safely out of their box. They are familiar with the platform of continued education (reading, listening, and conversing); however, there is a good chance that they have not been asked about it.

## Opening the Discussion

When your time is very limited with your customer, the dialogue probe is a very effective way to start a discussion. If you happen to have a customer who is available only for a couple of minutes, it is important to get to the point and generate interest to capture more time. The dialogue probe is especially useful when time is limited. Some of you reading this book may have as much time as several hours with your customer. On average, the typical sales call (excluding several industries) is about 30 to 40 minutes. If you have that much time, you can maneuver and pace yourself through the call with minimum pressure of spitting things out quickly. In the following chapters I talk about pacing the call. However, there are a handful of industries where time is extremely limited and precious. One of those industries is the pharmaceutical marketplace. When a drug representative calls on a doctor, the rep may only have a minute or two, or possibly less. If you are selling in that type of environment, the dialogue probing question is your answer.

## The Short Call

As a manufacturer's representative in the industrial, petrochemical and petroleum industry, many of my sales calls were extended. By this I mean that they were over 15 minutes in length. Actually, many of my calls lasted around an hour. My frame of reference was and has always been, "I have time for my customer." When I entered into the world of sales skill training, I was introduced to sales professionals and representatives who felt that they only have a minute or two to spend with the customer. In some cases less than a minute. My initial reaction was, wow, that is difficult. How do they get their point across and make a difference in that short amount of time? The dialogue probe is certainly useful for the extended call, but it is extremely effective for the short call as well.

## Timing

On average, a salesperson will try to "break the ice" with a customer at the beginning of the call (more on this later). If you have an extended call, this process can take up to several minutes. If you don't, the beginning of the call has to be managed very tightly. In the short-call scenario, the customer may be responsive to a bit of chitchat. But in other cases, maybe not. In any event, there will come a time in the short call, whether this is after a half minute or right out of the shoot, when the customer will say, "What do you have for me today?" or, "I am somewhat behind schedule. Make it quick." At first, the sales representative is put back on her heels. "What do I do? I only have a couple of seconds. I know. I'll go right to my presentation—that will work. My presentation (after all) is compelling." Wrong! Everyone's presentation is compelling, and if you don't capture the attention and intellectual interest of the customer, the presentation is lost and meaningless. There is a key to what I just said—capture the customer's *intellectual interest*.

If you go directly to your presentation, you have lost control. The customer is telling you where she wants you so she can allow you to speak and then manage you out. For the most part, if you go to the presentation, you are not gaining ground. Don't worry. A question will not offend your customer. The best thing you can do is ask him a question. But the key to success is that the question is all about the customer. When you make it all about customer, the clock is off, at least temporarily.

## The Clock Is Off

The clock is off when you focus on the customer. I would like to examine the "normal" (if such a designation is possible) short call. The customer opens up with quick chitchat or a "What do you have for me today?" routine. If you launch into a presentation, you will take about 30 seconds to describe your point. If you ask an open or closed question, you will take about 5 seconds. Here is my point: At times we waste time. When the customer says to you, "What do you have for me today?" or "Make it quick," a Pavlovian bell should be going off in your brain saying, "The customer is making me speed up things. I am going out of control." Seize the control back. How? By transitioning and asking a dialogue probing question. As soon as the customer says, "What do you have for me today?" transition quickly to, "I want to run a quick question by you." Probably, the customer will say, "Make it quick" (a little redundant).

At this moment deliver a dialogue probing question. It takes only about 10 to 12 seconds to deliver. Compared to the open probe which takes about 5 seconds, we are only asking for another 5 to 7 seconds. The dialogue probe will give you a better chance of captivating the interest and intellectual access of your customer. You are better off with a dialogue probe rather than with the same old presentation that the customer has heard numerous times before. If you deliver a dialogue probe in the short call, expect two responses. The first response will be a more detailed answer. Maybe the customer will actually say that it was a good question and proceed to answer it. If, for some reason, the question catches the customer off guard (even though you tried to soften the introduction of the question with your transition), the customer may respond with, "I don't have time to answer that question." Don't be alarmed. Simply deliver a quick point about your product or service and transition by asking, "Can you give me a couple of minutes the next time I am in to get your answer?" Transitioning in this way acknowledges the customer's request, yet at the same time you are giving yourself an opportunity to set up more time on the next call.

**6**

# Think Like
# Your Customer

## Talk and Think Like Your Customer:
## The Multilayered Probing Question

Ultimately, you want to be viewed as a partner, to be one of the chosen few who enters into the customer's "inner circle." The vendors in the inner circle are the ones that get most of the business. These are the people and companies the customer will trust more than any other supplier. Accessing the inner circle takes some time. Getting there can be made easier through the use of the multilayered probing question, or MLPQ.

The MLPQ is a question format that positions you as a peer. It mirrors the way most people obtain information, shows your level of knowledge and familiarity with the customer's interest, and gets the customer safely out of the box. This question type is different from the dialogue probe because of the way the question is structured. The MLPQ has the following three parts:

1.  Statement of fact
2.  Observation
3.  Probing question

## Part 1: Statement of Fact

Let's review each segment. The first segment is the statement of fact, which is responsible for entering into the conversation as a third-party source of information that will serve as the platform for the discussion. In simpler terms, once you open up your conversation and are several minutes into your meeting, use a multilayered question to elevate the discussion. The statement of fact plays an integral part in the effectiveness of this question type. The statement of fact is generated from a third-party source, which ideally should be a source that is not associated with your company: for example, articles from the *Wall Street Journal*, *Forbes*, or *Business Week*, or a report from CNBC. The purpose of the statement of fact is to introduce a topic of interest to the customer, such as improving return on investments, office productivity, health-care costs, or employee productivity. Introducing a topic through a proven third-party source enables you to provide the customer with undisputed information to consider. A statement of fact may sound something like this: "Mr. Customer, the other day I was reading an article in the *Wall Street Journal* and thought about your company. The article was on the ever-increasing issue of health-care costs and ways to contain them. The article said . . . " I think you are getting the picture. The statement of fact introduces information to get the customer out of the box. Because the information comes from a third-party source, it is deemed as credible. If, for some reason, the customer does not agree with the information, she is disagreeing with the source and not with you. This enables you to maintain your relationship and avoid any problems. The use of the third-party news source is to help you initiate a different conversation. Other sources for the statement of fact include reliable Internet or Web site sources, reports, studies, or excerpts from expert speakers. On occasion, the statement of fact can have its limits in several industries in which a company and its sales representatives can use only "approved" material. This approved material could be a study, information on the company Web site, or information that the company prepares about the product or service it offers.

Whether you have free rein to outsource any reliable avenue of information or you are completely restricted to one or two sources, the format of the MLPQ is valuable. It is especially valuable if you are limited in your ability to get new information. For example, if your customer has heard over and over again about your study or sales aid, the statement of fact can breathe new life into something that is old. Recently a student in my class said to me that she was able to use only one proof source during her presentations. She explained that it got very boring for the customer, but the introduction of the MLPQ format provided new options. I asked her to explain what she meant. She said that her article had about two thousand sentences. In a new and invigorating tone, she said, "That could be two thousand statements of fact." If you happen to fall into this category of a restricted number of proof sources, the following transition would be helpful to introduce your statement of fact: "Ms. Customer, for weeks (or maybe even months) we have been talking about the Brown article (proof source), and I would like to circle back to a particular point that I think you will find very interesting. The article went on to suggest . . ."

If you have limited-to-no restrictions on the source for your statement of fact, you have an endless fountain of information for wowing your customer. Knowledge in this case is what can separate you from your competitors. If you keep introducing new, pertinent, and informative data on an ongoing basis, you will be viewed as having more value. Bringing value is a determining factor in who receives ongoing access and limitless time.

Every once in a while you might have to wait a few minutes to see a customer, and you are told that the customer can only spare a few minutes of time. While you are waiting, another salesperson walks into the office, schmoozes with the staff, and pops in ahead of you. That person takes what seems to be forever and walks out the door while you are still standing there waiting to see the customer. That, ladies and gentlemen, is the salesperson who is in the inner circle. The MLPQ will help you get there. The following list provides many ideas for sources of the statement of fact:

1. *Wall Street Journal*
2. *New York Times*
3. *USA Today*
4. Major city newspapers such as the *Philadelphia Inquirer, Los Angeles Times, Boston Globe,* or the *Chicago Tribune*
5. *Newsweek* magazine
6. *Forbes* magazine
7. MSNBC
8. CNN
9. Credible Web sites, such as WebMD, that offer medical advice
10. Industry conference speaker excerpts and reports
11. Studies, reports, surveys, assessments

Opening up your discussion with a statement of fact allows you to separate yourself from others and suggests that you have done your research and are offering more value. When the statement of fact is delivered, the customer can respond to a specific point of reference. Delivering the statement of fact in the proper way is important. For years, I supported the introduction of the statement of fact and a recital of what was indicated in the article or proof source. An example of the introduction of the proof source would be, "The other day I was reading an article in the *Wall Street Journal* about the increasing need to diversify your portfolio now more than ever. The article stated . . ."

For years I taught that format, and the format worked. But recently, as a client's legal department was reviewing our seminar content, a new option revealed itself to me. During our content review process, I received a phone call from the company's lawyer requesting that I reformat an MLPQ example from the workbook. When I located the MLPQ question under review, I said to the lawyer: "I don't understand. I am using the exact same wording from an approved study that you provide your sales representatives. What seems to be the problem?" The lawyer said that the statement of fact had a conclusion. I responded back to the lawyer that his comment was correct and that the conclusion originated from the client's own study. Unwavering, the lawyer said: "That may be the case, but we can't say concluded; we have to say suggested." I told the lawyer that I would make the change. I hung up the phone and thought to myself: "Whatever!" A few weeks passed, and the revised workbooks for the session in question were completed. During the course of the program, I introduced the MLPQ technique and instructed the group on the importance of ending the statement of fact by saying, "The article went on to suggest . . ." At that moment it hit me: "Yes, that's it!" All these years we have been saying "The article concluded . . ." When you say that to your customer, you are painting a very vivid black or white picture. There is no room for gray.

However, when you say, "the article suggested . . . ," it leaves the door open for intense discussion. So every once in a while, lawyers are helpful. Therefore, end the statement of fact with, "The article went on to suggest . . ." This gives you more of an opportunity to start a discussion.

## Part 2: Observation

The second part of the MLPQ question is the observation. The observation's primary role is to lend greater support and validity to the statement of fact. The observation is to bolster the statement of fact by lending more information about its authenticity. The sources for the observation can be the same as the aforementioned list for proof sources; however, the preferred delivery is to select a different proof source from the statement of fact. The following is an example of this:

*Statement of fact:* The other day I was reading an article in the *Wall Street Journal* about the increasing need to diversify your portfolio now more than ever. The article went on to suggest. . .

*Observation:* In a separate article in *Forbes*, the same idea was emphasized.

Supporting the *Wall Street Journal* article with the *Forbes* article lends more credibility to the statement of fact. Another way of lending support is to back up the statement of fact with a complementary comment that might originate from an industry expert. A similar example of this could be a speaker from a conference. The observation could come from information from a good source on the Web. The combination of two different proof sources gives more traction to the statement of fact. At times, I have been approached about the order of the statement of fact and observation. Can the observation come first and the statement of fact second? Yes. The application, in any combination, of the statement of fact and observation helps you bring value.

### Part 3: The Probe

The last part of the MLPQ is the probe. This is the piece that ties it all together. Without the probe, the question loses impact. For the most part, the third part of this question is a minidialogue probe. Once the statement of fact and observation are introduced, it is your job to connect them to the customer. Connecting the fact and observation to the customer is actually pretty easy. As a matter of fact, don't overthink this part. The probe is simply, "Please share with me what you are experiencing in your (department, company, practice) and how it compares to what the article is suggesting." There is that word again, suggesting. Short and sweet. What are you experiencing compared to what the article is saying? There is no right or wrong. The question is safe to answer and educates the customer at the same time. There is no need to get fancy here. Sure, you can put the probe in your own words, but basically the question is what is the customer experiencing and how does it compare to the proof sources that you introduced?

## Educating and Engaging

The overriding purpose of the MLPQ is to educate and engage the customer at the same time. It is to give the customer new and different information to allow her to percolate the information and determine how it compares to what she is seeing. In some industries, the customer base is very familiar with this format (fact, observation, and probe) because this is how the people are taught. In some industries, the customer (in the pursuit of his educational degree) is required to source third-party information to support his theories. Linking into the way some of your customers have been educated will provide them with a familiar and comfortable question that they are used to. It will also enable you to blend in with them.

## Adjusting the MLPQ to the Customer

Earlier, I introduced the topic of communication and personality styles. The customer's personality style should be considered when crafting and delivering an MLPQ, so you should adjust based on the customer's personality styles. When you edit the MLPQ based on the customer's personality styles, only the observation and the probing question are affected. For the most part, the statement of fact remains intact.

Table 6.1 provides direction for constructing the MLPQ.

| Personality Style | Observation | Probing Question |
|---|---|---|
| Controller customer | Delete the observation. Deliver a statement of fact and probe. | The probing question is recommended as, "Tell me your experience and how it compares to the article's suggestion." |
| Amiable customer | Observation should indicate where other colleagues and thought leaders are onboard. | The probing question is recommended as, "Share with me your experience and how it compares to what seems to be a trend." |

| Analytical customer | Analytical personalities tend to prefer stats, figures, and numbers. In both the statement of fact and observation, offer as much proof as possible. This personality style would suggest the delivery of two statements of fact, full of information. | The probing question is suggested as, "Tell me your thoughts on this data and how it compares with what the articles are suggesting." |
|---|---|---|
| Expressive customer | • Appreciates new, different, and unusual information<br>• Likes to be positioned as the "authority"<br>• Wants to express own views | The probing question is suggested as, "Explain to me your experience and how it compares with what the articles are suggesting." |

TABLE **6.1** Editing the MLPQ

# 7

# How to Hear
# What Others Don't

This chapter provides insight into what to do once the customer answers a dialogue, multilayered, or open or closed probing question. Once you ask a better question, the next task or challenge is learning what to do with the customer's answer. One of the keys in separating yourself from your competition is to better understand what the customer is experiencing. Many years ago I remember reading a quote, "People buy when they feel understood." This is true in business and certainly true in personal relationships. So the better you can communicate, the more revealing and comfortable the other person will become with you. One of the leading reasons relationships fail is because of the individuals' lack of communication skills.

## Carrying on a Conversation

Carrying on a conversation is something of a lost art. I would like to describe a scenario that most of us have faced in our adult life. I am referring to the dreaded mandatory party that your spouse, significant other, or family member drags you to, and you don't know anyone there. Sound familiar? Personally, I am not a big fan of such a situation, but it is possible to manage it and have a positive experience.

A few years back, my wife and I were invited to a "class party." It was at the beginning of the school year, near the end of September. The purpose of the party was to provide a chance for all of the students' parents to meet one another. On the surface, it sounds like a great idea. It makes sense to meet the parents of the children your son or daughter hangs out with. Unfortunately, it can be a real burden if your child is in a new school, and you don't know anyone. Sound familiar? Faced with this situation a number of years ago, I tried to get myself out of attending the party. I had no good excuses or reasons to avoid the party. It was a Saturday night, and I was faced with an evening where, if I weren't conversational, it might make for a difficult night. I didn't want to don my sales hat initially, but after a couple of minutes of deliberation, I decided it would be the best thing for me to do.

When we arrived at the party, I was glad to see a good offering of beverages—including my favorite drink—and, most importantly, good food. This was a plus; at least I would be well fed. Therefore, the trick is how to be conversational and eat at the same time. If you have tried to do this, you know it is a balancing act. You can't talk with your mouth full—right?

## Putting the Plan into Action

I put my plan into action: First, a trip to the bar to get my drink; second, grab some of that good food; and third, start a lengthy conversation—the most difficult task. I maneuvered myself around the room until I found the hostess of the party, a very nice person. I complimented her on the presentation of the food and her home and then put the plan into action. (I had a cold drink and warm food and didn't want that to be reversed!) After I complimented her, I asked where she and her husband were from originally. I knew to ask this because I'd learned that their child was new to the school. Learning they were from the Midwest, I was faced with the dreaded lull in the conversation and went to work. I transitioned by commenting what a great area the Midwest is and asking how long she lived there. She told me. I could have changed the focus and told her about the times I had lived in Chicago to see if we had any similar stories, but I didn't. Deciding to keep the discussion going and to maintain the focus on her, I asked if that is where she had met her husband and how they had met. This might seem too personal, but it isn't. Why? Because people love to tell that story. And, for the most part the story starts with, "Oh, my gosh, it is such a funny story." While she finished answering the question, I had consumed my cold drink and eaten my warm food. I listened intently, shook my head a couple of times to acknowledge I was listening, and told her it was a great story. Mission accomplished, fed, and hydrated, I had listened to her story and come across as a good guy! Why? Because I kept the focus on her. The same must apply to selling.

## Keep the Focus on the Customer

Every so often, in our attempt to align and find common ground with an individual, we unknowingly take over the conversation. Think of the last time you were in a discussion about a vacation destination. As the other person told you about his trip to a place that you also had visited, did you become eager to share your story too? It is okay in a social setting, but not in the world of sales. It is essential to keep the focus on the customer. To accomplish this, I recommend a couple of different ways to listen to an individual. Figure 7.1 provides a "conversation flow chart" that will enable you to uncover more information. The chart

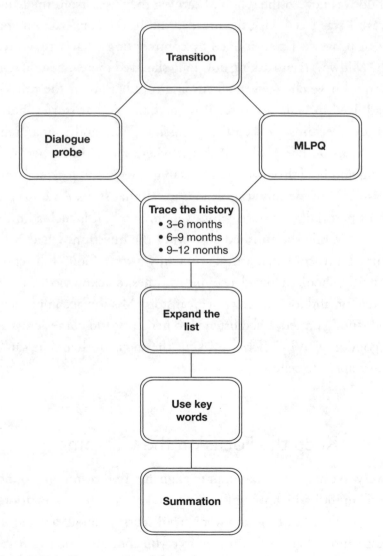

**Figure 7.1** Conversational flow chart.

introduces several new listening concepts: Trace the History, Expand the List, and Key Words.

Each of these techniques is independent of the others. They can, however, fit nicely into a listening algorithm that provides a map for listening and carrying a conversation. This chapter shares with you how to avoid the common pitfalls in a sales conversation and enhance your ability to listen and carry on a conversation. In addition, this chapter provides insight on how to identify the spoken and unspoken word and sharpen your ability to hear what others can't. Knowing how to discern the intent of the customer, staying focused on the issues, and creating an environment that is conducive to complete disclosure will assist in your ability to obtain sensitive, confidential, and little-talked-about information.

## Getting the Conversation Started

The first task in getting a conversation started is to ask a good dialogue or multilayered probing question (MLPQ). Asking for a dialogue or MLPQ helps get the customer to stop, think, and respond with a different answer. Once that is accomplished, there is the need to "work" and nurture the answer. The challenge is whether you can get more from the answer and further separate you from the next guy. It is our hope that by asking a dialogue or multilayered question, you will have a head start in the conversation category. To gain more insight, I'd like to share with you some ideas about these three advanced listening concepts.

### *Trace the History*

By far, one of my favorite things to do is to trace the history of a person's response. Every answer has a past—some good, some not so good. It is your job to uncover more information. The story that opened this chapter about the cocktail party was an example of tracing the history. In social settings, tracing the history can generate a wealth of information. For example, tracing the history is particularly useful when you're talking with individuals about their interests and hobbies. A social setting is a good place to practice this concept before you use it on your customers. During a conversation, people often will reveal their enjoyment of tennis, skiing, golf, the arts, basketball, cooking, and so on. At times we will get into a banter of peripheral questions like, "Where do you like to ski?" "What do you like to cook?" "Do you play singles or doubles (tennis)?" "Who is your favorite artist?" These fact-finding questions have merit and generate some additional information about the person's hobby and interests. I encourage these information-gathering questions. However, once you have asked the informational questions and the canvas is ready, you can trace the history.

For example, you can begin by asking, "Can you share with me when you first became interested in cooking (or skiing, tennis, the arts, etc.)?" You can see how this may take a person back years or maybe even decades. You are going from the present all the way back to the fairly distant past. To paraphrase Shakespeare, the past is prologue. The past can uncover hidden treasures of information. The follow-up question once the history question is asked and answered could be, "Do you remember how you first became interested in cooking (golf, tennis, etc.)?" If the topics of golf or cooking were discussed, our research shows that the number one response to this question is either mother or father. These answers can open up an entirely new conversation about the times spent with those individuals. I believe you are getting the picture.

For the most part, up to 90 percent of our questions and conversations deal with the present and the future. The goal for this component of the conversation is to see if you can get more information about the past. Take a look at some of the questions that you ask your customers. Where do they fall—past, present, or future? Even if you have a couple of questions that fall under the past category, I would like you to heighten your awareness of going to the customer's history or past more often. Taking a trip down memory lane might get a customer to realize the need to get out of the box. Many of the ideas presented in this book are keys to getting the customer out of that box.

### How Far Back Is Appropriate?

For the most part, there are no limits in social conversation. Sometimes going all the way back to their initial involvement with something can be good. But that is not always the case with your customer or prospective customer. If you happen to go too far back in time, your customer may respond with a curt answer that may be something like, "I can't even remember what I did last week, let alone five years ago!" This is not the answer you want.

For the business timeline, there are three suggested time frames and one exception. The suggested time frames are shown in Figure 7.1, but they need not always be discussed in strict linear chronological order. At times, a history-tracing conversation might even proceed in reverse chronological order, as follows:

9–12 months
6–9 months
3–6 months

The time frames shown in Figure 7.1 seem to work best with customers by presenting them with a frame of reference that is reasonable to recall. Going too far into the past might not be as useful. By getting customers to trace their history, you are hoping to mine useful information and at the same time get the customer thinking about change. If you can get the customer to recall what has been happening in her unit, floor, practice, operation, and so on over the last six to nine months, the customer may realize that something is happening more often than she would like. If you feel that your customer has somewhat of a short attention span and memory, select the shorter time frame of three to six months. If you feel that your customer may have an intermediate memory, go for the six- to nine-month time frame. And if you think you have a customer who is like an elephant and never forgets anything, go for the long time span of 9 to 12 months.

### *Using the Information to Your Advantage*
When tracing the history, use the information to your advantage and position the question well. For example, if you are trying to replace an incumbent, a review of the customer's history may reveal a couple of speed bumps along the way that would open the door for change. If, on the other hand, you are discussing a problem with your product and you are trying to manage an objection or obstacle, there is no need to amplify it by tracing the customer's disappointment and frustration for the past 12 months. Tracing the history is like a pause button on your CD player; it allows you to get caught up with the information, and it slows down the conversation to better enable you to understand the origin of the customer's answer. Tracing the history gives you and the customer the opportunity to absorb and explore the information being discussed. It gives you a chance to slow things down and really listen.

The only anomaly that disrupts tracing the history or the suggested timelines of 3–6, 6–9, or 9–12 months is if an adverse or unexpected event occurred in a customer's industry or marketplace that would be considered a milestone or change in direction. If that is the situation, it is appropriate to trace back to that point in time. An example of this could be a correction of the stock market or economy, or the unexpected introduction of a revolutionary new technology or product.

## Expand the List

Step one on the map to creating a better conversation is to trace the history of the customer's response. Step two is to expand the list—that is, to purposefully enlarge the scope of the discussion. Much like the notion that every response has a history, the same is true with reference to expanding the list.

A number of years ago, I realized that a growing number of business discussions stay within the boundaries of the customer's agenda. The customer will send out a request for proposal (RFP). In this request, the customer outlines what he wants done and expects vendors to submit their proposals and pricing. The problem with this is that the playing field is too level. You are all submitting your solution based on the same information and prerequisites. It is your job to expand the scope of the discussion to tilt the playing field in your favor. If you happen to be the incumbent, you might have an edge in the selection process because people don't like to change. Recently, I conducted a discovery process with a prospective customer, while discussing his needs and the impact of schema in his industry, he reported that prospective clients believe that the cost of change is troublesome. Well put and worth repeating. The cost of change is troublesome.

## Tilt the Field in Your Direction

One method of gathering more information than the competition is to acknowledge and listen for "the list." Most, if not all, of a person's answer will come from a list of choices. Let's start with some of the more obvious lists: favorite color or ice cream. Each of these categories provides many options. If we were to ask an individual what her favorite flavor of ice cream is, she would answer. What we didn't get her to divulge was all of the other flavors that were under consideration. For example, the person answers, "Cookies and cream." (A good choice, I may add!) If she deliberated over the answer, she probably was processing her choices before giving her final answer. When an individual takes time to answer a question, this is an indication that she is processing her choices before responding. The person did not say, "Vanilla, chocolate, strawberry, or rocky road." However, she might have processed those selections en route to giving her answer. The same is true with your customer. She will process and, at times, selectively respond. It is your job to expand the list—meaning, find out the other choices she was considering.

Let us return to social discussions with friends and family members before we center on our customers. When we talk to a friend about his favorite sport, he might tell you tennis. When you receive that answer, don't rule out that he might be interested in or involved in other activities. Tennis may be his preference because of the group of people he plays with, the league he is in, or the fact that he can play year-round (indoor and outdoor). Your friend may also like skiing but doesn't get a chance to do it as often; therefore, it is not top of mind, like tennis.

## Top of Mind

The customer will reveal what is at the "top of her mind." In some cases, she selectively gives you some information and leaves out other pieces of information. The information she leaves out and the information underneath her top of mind is what you are after. If you can obtain this information, if it exists, you will be far ahead of the competition. To review, you will be told by the customer what she wants you to hear. What she shares with you will be important. That information will provide the basis for the discussion and give you preliminary information about her needs. However, if you don't go beyond this information, you will be cast into the same pool as everyone else, swimming in the same information, presenting the same solution, and, for the most part, offering the same price.

Make a difference in the conversation by expanding the list. When a person gives you an answer, it is essential to acknowledge the answer and realize there is probably just as much information that is unsaid. Therefore, the need exists to trace the history and expand the customer's list.

### Acknowledge and Expand

To make this work, you need to acknowledge and expand the list. For example, you are in a discussion with a prospective customer, and you ask a dialogue question. The customer tells you that you have asked an interesting question and replies: "I haven't thought about it that way. I guess my main concern is to reduce the cost of our operation." Good job. The main concern was revealed. Chances are that several other salespeople that compete with you have also obtained that information. But there may still be some information to be had. The recommended approach to expanding the list is as follows: "Mr. or Ms. Customer, you responded to my question by identifying reduction of costs of your operation. I would like to focus on and spend time on what led you to say that and to gain a full understanding of this issue" (setting up the trace-the-history question), "but before I do that, can you share with me some of the other areas you may have evaluated before you identified the need to reduce costs?"

If you can get another element into the discussion, for example, improving employee morale, you now can craft your proposal to address two issues instead of one. If your competition is addressing one issue and you are addressing two, you have the better solution. The better solution is worth more money, right? In a sense, you are killing two needs with one proposal.

Get comfortable with expanding the list. Practice with a friend. If he tells you he likes tennis, tell him you would like to hear all about it; tell him that it's a great sport, but ask if there are other areas that interest him. This question can open up a few more doors. This question allows you to maintain focus on the first answer (which is important) and possibly gain additional insight into other areas of interest. If you accomplish this, you are viewed as more intuitive, and you have a better sense of what this customer wants done.

### Avoid the Trap

At times, your eagerness to expand the list can appear to be counterproductive. If you do not acknowledge the original answer, assuring the customer that you will cover the topic in detail and then turn to another topic, it may appear that you are not listening. If this occurs, it could be damaging. Expanding the list is about getting more information. A bad example of expanding the list would be, "You mentioned the reduction of cost in your operation; what other areas are important to you?" This question sends mixed messages. The customer is thinking, "What just happened? You asked me a question. I gave you the answer, and you disregarded it." This is a valid point. Therefore, make sure the expand-the-list technique is applied properly.

If you are involved in a conversation that is longer than 15 minutes, you will be able to ask a dialogue question—possibly a multilayered question—trace the history, and expand the list all in one call. If, however, your calls or conversations are much shorter, you need a game plan. Prior to your call or telephone call, make a decision about which question you will open with and which listening technique you will employ. If you have a brief amount of time, select either the trace-the-history or expand-the-list technique. The delivery of both may be over-whelming. And, if you have a series of short calls with the cus-tomer, you can set up or piggyback each of the techniques. For example, if during your first contact you traced the history, you can start out the second contact with a quick recap and move into expanding the list. The concepts in this book, along with the content in our live and Web-based seminars, provide great flexibility. We are providing you with the tools. Based on the job at hand, you will determine the techniques that you feel will be appropriate to implement.

## Key Words

Earlier I made a reference to Barbara Walters and her ability to get individuals to reveal hard-to-get and even confidential informa-tion. Some other individuals in the media possess similar skills to get people to open up. The concepts of tracing the history and expanding the list will serve you in your efforts to get more infor-mation. The final concept of this chapter is the one that will get people to open up on another level. The last piece of the listening map, key words, will help you to get the customer to open up on an emotional level. Making this happen correctly takes some prac-tice and a careful sense of what is and what isn't appropriate.

We all say them. But we might not hear them. Key words can be obvious, but more often they are hidden. In sales, there is a tendency to listen for what we want to hear. When we hear it, we perceive that information as the green light to start selling. For example, when the customer says he needs to reduce the cost of his operations, we plunge into our presentation and tell him how we are a great partner to accomplish that task. As we found out in this chapter, if we sprint to the presentation or solution, we might be leaving some important information buried. Digging up uncovered information can make the difference between having a special or an ordinary business relationship. This could be the difference in getting more business or not. Key words can make a difference.

### Be Patient When You Listen

A fun example I conduct in my live classes is to determine whether the students can hear what the person is saying and identify what wasn't said. I use as an example an interview that was conducted with Donald Trump. The topic of discussion centered on his finances. The interviewer asked, "One of the ways to reduce debt is to sell assets. Which asset or assets are you willing to sell?" He responded: "I may sell parts of my assets. I may sell a percentage of my casinos, my hotels, or my airline, which is doing really well."

When I share this question and response to my class participants, I ask them to compose a follow-up question to continue the conversation. Some of the answers I have heard are: "Which asset would you sell first?" "Why would you sell an asset that is doing well?" "Why would you sell a percentage and not a whole asset?" I tell them that these are all reasonable follow-up questions, although in some cases, the answers to them could be somewhat pedestrian. Then I explain that the group may have missed one of the most important and key words of his response. Right around this part of the exercise I get a bunch of puzzled looks that say, "Go on. Tell us what we missed."

The first words out of the Donald's mouth were very revealing. And in normal conversation we tend to miss the first words in a person's response. As a culture, we are tuned in to listening to the last thing people say and carry the conversation from that point on. But, every so often, we disregard the first thing people say. Donald Trump said: "I may sell parts of assets. I may sell a percentage of my casinos, hotels, or airline." If Donald Trump says "I may," it also means "I may not." But for the most part people hear the end of the answer and carry the conversation forward. And, from Trump's point of view, he may be thinking: "I don't think you heard me," or worse, "I don't think you understand my position." This can be damaging. To prevent this from happening, take your time. You've asked your question. Listen to the answer. All too often we are concerned about time or delivering a great presentation. In some cases, we can't wait to give our answer. We love to hear ourselves talk. (Did I just say that?)

### Pace Yourself

Customers will give you all the clues you need—just listen for them. If Donald Trump says, "I may," it could mean that there is some uncertainty. Instead of launching into questions about which asset, what percentage, as the interviewer did, it might be better suited to say, "Donald, it sounds like you have given this some consideration and there might be a level of uncertainty as to which way to go. Could you share with me your thoughts on your response?" Nine out of ten times, that is a killer follow-up question.

**Words that convey certainty . . .**
Always
Never
All
Every

**Words that convey uncertainty . . .**
May
Often
Frequently
Few
Some

These words may provide a clue to what is going on behind the scenes. If you can open up the emotional can of worms in your favor, you are making progress. I am not asking you to be a psychologist. I am not suggesting that the customer needs to lie down on a couch, but do take a page out of the therapist's book. Psychologists are very deliberate. They are paid to listen. Sometimes it is annoying because of the repetitive nature of their questions. We do not want to be annoying or redundant, but there is information out there for the taking. Take your time with the customer's answer. He processed his response; therefore, you need to process and dissect his answer. Pull it apart carefully. What, if any, are the key words that were stated in his answer? What is his list and how far back does the history go? Getting this information will allow you to build a stronger business relationship and a solution presentation.

*Interpreting*
Just as a visitor from another country needs someone to interpret words into her own language to understand what is happening in a discussion, you may need to do the same with your customer.

Sometimes the customer does speak in a foreign language. If you can decipher her code, you can gain valuable information.

There is a balance and sensitivity required with deciphering key words. If you misinterpret, you could cause a problem. Choosing your words and responses carefully is essential in this step. Exploring key words is somewhat of an art. You first have to hear the key word, and then you have to interpret the word and its context.

When you elect the path of "key words," be careful. Phrase your response in an acceptable form that does not create a negative tone. Do choose your words carefully, circle back to the key word you identified, and ask the customer to tell you more about that choice of word. If necessary, transition by saying, "You used the word 'may' in your answer about selling assets. That word could indicate you have been giving this some thought; it might suggest that you are trying to determine which path or direction would be the best to take, but at this time there is a level of uncertainty. Could you tell me more about your answer?"

A careful, thoughtful, and deliberate question surrounding a customer's choice of words should be well received. A rapid-fire response such as, "You used the word 'may'; it sounds like you don't know what you are going to do," would elicit a negative response. Applying this skill requires time, so I would not suggest its application for the short call or the difficult customer. Save this for when you have time with the customer and for when you've become more proficient. The concept of key words requires a more cerebral approach. Rushing through or forcing this skill will cause it to fail. Pick your spots. It is okay to be inquisitive to get your customer to go into more detail about the selection of his words and the tone of his response.

If you identify key words in the customer's response and your questions do not provide any additional information, it is okay.

You tried and found out that his choice of words did not have any additional meaning. However, if you do uncover additional meaning, you are that much farther ahead.

## Summation

Whether you are involved in the short or the extended call, I recommend that you include a quick recap, or summation, before moving into the presentation or solution phase of your sales call or contact. A summation is most appropriate in longer sales calls. A more detailed discussion focusing on pacing the sales call appears in Chapter 8.

Once you have asked a dialogue or multilayered question and implemented any or all of the advanced listening skills outlined in this chapter, it is important to summarize and even prioritize the customer's answer. Crafting a summary and prioritizing the customer's answers are not new. However, the inclusion of tracing the history, expanding the list, and identifying the customer's key words can produce new and robust answers. Summarizing all the information that has been gathered and prioritizing its importance will help focus you and the customer for the rest of the call.

**For the short call . . .**
Dialogue probe
Trace the history or expand the list

**For the extended call . . .**
Multilayered question and/or dialogue probe
Trace the history
Expand the list
Identify key words
Give a summary

## Personal Use Recommended

This chapter is designed for the application of advanced listening skills with your customer. These skills also have great application as life skills for everyday use. When appropriate, you can trace the history of a friend's response, expand the list of a neighbor, or delve into the selection of key words by a family member. You never know what you might learn.

# 8

# Are You Creating a Flow in Your Conversation?

How many times have you been managed in and out of a customer's office? Probably more times than you would like to remember—right? Or how often has the customer started the call by saying, "So what do you have for me today?" As soon as you hear that, you get the sense that the customer is trying to get you in and get you out of the office fast. Primarily, the customer's main emphasis is to listen quickly to what you have to say and get you out of the office or workspace.

Everyone knows the importance of getting the call off to a good start, establishing a nice flow to the conversation, managing expectations, and seeking closure at the end of the conversation. This chapter introduces a model to assist you in making this happen more often. The *quarter/half/quarter model* is an easy-

131

to-use visual model to help you pace and control a conversation. Using this model will enable you to determine exactly where you are in the conversation, where you need to be, and where the customer is trying to take you.

## How the Model Was Developed

A number of years ago, while I was teaching a group of accountants how to generate more business, I attempted to describe for them the importance of opening the conversation at the beginning of the contact, presenting a solution halfway through the conversation, and gaining commitment at the end of the call. I suggested that the sales call contain all three events and follow a sequential order or flow. In my mind it was simple; all you had to do were three things: Open up the call and ask questions, present your offerings by resolving the client's concerns or issues, and close.

As easy as that sounds, many of the accountants in the group struggled with the notion of including all of these things during a meeting with a prospective client. They couldn't conceptually grasp what I was saying. Sales were not something they embraced. In some cases, it was the last thing some of the managers wanted to do. They preferred working with numbers, not calling on clients. After I explained the need to include all three parts in every conversation with a prospective client, one of the participants raised his hand with a question. With somewhat of a confused look on his face he asked, "Charlie, could you diagram for us what you are talking about?" I hesitated for a moment to process the request. I was somewhat surprised with the question, because this was second nature to me. But I quickly realized that most of the participants in the class had limited sales experience and were of an analytical nature. After all, they were accountants and, in their minds, not salespeople. I agreed.

After a brief pause to think of the best way to explain this, I asked each person in the class to take out a blank sheet of paper. I told them to draw a circle in the middle of the paper, and to view the circle as if it were a clock face. I told them to draw a straight line from nine o'clock to three o'clock. As I was making this request, I was drawing the diagram on the flip chart that was in front of the room to demonstrate what it looked like. After I drew the bisected circle, I stepped back and took a look at what I had just drawn: a circle cut in half from left to right by a line from nine o'clock to three o'clock. (See Figure 8.1.)

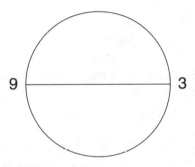

**FIGURE 8.1** Circle divided into halves.

I then asked the group to draw a vertical line from twelve o'clock to the line they just drew. Once again, I stepped back to look at the drawing, which now consisted of a circle divided into three parts. These three parts were to represent the three steps that I mentioned to them earlier. I paused again to look at the circle and then instructed the group to identify each of the sections. I asked them to label the first section from twelve o'clock to three o'clock as the first quarter. I then instructed them to go the largest section of the circle (the portion under the three o'clock to nine o'clock line). I told them to label this section the half. And finally, I asked them to classify the last section of the drawing, the segment from nine o'clock back up to twelve o'clock, as the last quarter. (See Figure 8.2.)

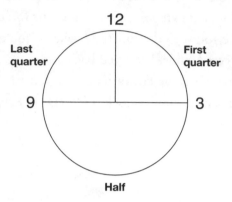

**FIGURE 8.2** Circle divided into three portions: the basic quarter/half/quarter model.

The quarter/half/quarter model was born right in front of me. Out of a level of frustration came a simple, easy-to-follow visual model to pace and control a sales call. The model was an uncomplicated approach to selling. It could be used for face-to-face sales calls. It could be applied to phone conversations. It could be used for a short call or an extended call. There was no need to memorize a bunch of steps and flow charts with arrows. It was straightforward. It suggested that every sales call or conversation had three parts. It did not matter whether the conversation took place with one person or many. It still consisted of three parts. It did not matter what type of customer you were calling on: frequent, moderate, or occasional. It did not matter whether the customer liked her job or whether you were talking with the executive in the corner office or the supervisor of a project over the hood of a pickup truck. The parts remain the same. How you execute the parts is a whole different story.

## Pacing the Call

The quarter/half/quarter model is designed to pace and control a conversation. It can help you to know where you are in the conversation and gauge where you need to be. The model is an indication of the things you have to accomplish and the time required to do it. For the most part, you open the call, establish a business relationship, present a solution, and close. Therefore, moving clockwise through the model, the labels for each section of the quarter/half/quarter model are as follows:

First quarter—opener
Half—build the business relationship
Last quarter—present a solution and close

This is diagrammed in Figure 8.3.

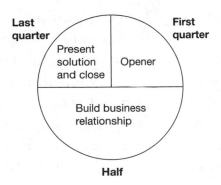

**FIGURE 8.3** The quarter/half/quarter model with descriptions.

The quarter/half/quarter model is also an indicator of how to spend your time. Each section name suggests the amount of time that should be spent in each part. When you are opening the conversation, no more than 25 percent of your time should be spent in the first quarter. Regardless of whether your opener has a formal or more casual tone, your time in this section should not exceed 25 percent of the time you spend with your customer. For example, if you have an hour with your customer, you cannot spend more than 15 minutes reminiscing about the big game on Saturday or how well your child played at the soccer tournament. If you exceed the designated time limit, you may be wasting time. Note that this book is not about getting to know the customer on a personal basis—you should know how to do that already. This is about getting an edge with an existing customer and driving the relationship to a deeper, more prolific level.

The same is true for the other sections. The half part of the model should take up half of your time with the customer. In my opinion, this is the most important part of the model. This is the part of the conversation/sales call where you engage the customer and build a stronger business relationship. The purpose of this section of the model is to enable you to capture more information than your competitor. This is where you will use dialogue, multilayered probing questions, trace the history, expand the list, and identify key word techniques. This is the section that separates you from the rest. Consequently, if you have an hour with the customer, allow around 30 minutes to complete this portion of the model. If for some reason, you are cut short and can't ask all the questions you want and gather all the information that you need, you are now aware that this section of the model is being compromised. Half the battle is acknowledging that a short circuit is occurring. If you know you are being rushed through this section or any section of the model, you can get back to it at another time, complete the process, and stay on track.

## The Half—
## The Most Important Section

The half is the most important section of the model. As your business relationship forms with the customer, this is the section that will pay the most dividends. In this section, you are attempting to uncover more information and engage your customer in dialogue. This is the part of the sales call where you want to generate new thought, discover new information, and raise the level of discussion to create intellectual access and complex thinking. This cannot occur if this section of the model is rushed or forced. Being successful in this section of the model is incumbent upon your preparing good questions and knowing how to carry a conversation. If you can successfully execute the use of the dialogue and multilayered questions, trace the history, expand the list, and identify key words in the half part of the model, you are heading in the right direction for gathering more intelligence than the next person.

Following the quarter/half/quarter model helps you know where you are in the sales call and avoid the trap of "showing up and throwing up." This term refers to spilling your beans in the lobby. You tell the customer everything about the product before she has an interest in knowing what your product or service can do. If the sales call or conversation with the customer is longer than an hour, the actual time spent in each section of the model can be left up to your discretion. For example, if you happen to spend two hours with the customer in a sales call, I am not suggesting that you could be in the opener for 30 minutes. The model is a guide to help you improve the pacing and impact of each and every one of your conversations. It is a barometer for measuring how well things are moving along. Are things moving too quickly; or are they going too slowly? The percentages of 25/50/25 are also a guide to let you know that you should not be spending more than 25 percent of your time in the opening and closing sections or 50 percent in the half section. If you spend too much time in a certain section of the model, you may not be able to accomplish the other tasks that are required to develop and further the business relationship. In a sense, the quarter/half/quarter model is a two-edged sword. It tells you how much time you should spend in each section, and it presents itself as an administrator to prevent you from spending too much time in any of the three sections.

But what if you have only a couple of minutes to talk with your customer? If that is the case, the time segments in each component get reduced dramatically. The model is suggesting that you spend a nominal amount of time in the opener and that more time should be spent focused on the half, the part of the model that makes the difference. This is the section that helps you gain an edge over the competition. It is okay to check in with your customer at the beginning of the call if time is of the essence (especially if you have an established relationship and know more about his life and what he does outside of work). I don't mean that you need to say, "How are the kids? Great," and move on. However, the work of differentiating and separation is done in the half part of the model. Keep in mind, the opener is not the main emphasis of the call.

Relationships are developed by what happens in the half part of the model; therefore, the half part should take the most time.

If you happen to have an hour with your customer, try to use 30 minutes of your time utilizing what is presented in Chapter 5 about asking questions and Chapter 6 about listening and carrying a conversation. If you happen to have less time, maybe around 10 minutes, then make sure 5 of those minutes are spent asking better questions and listening. The quarter/half/quarter model will give you balance and direction.

## The Last Quarter

The last section of the model is where you present your solution and close. Time spent in this section will depend on the progression of the relationship. At first, the time spent in this section (presenting solutions and closing) may be limited. The actual time may be around 25 percent of your time or less. As you make subsequent calls and you gather more data and information, it will be more appropriate to spend more time in the last quarter. The emphasis will shift from the half to the last quarter as your relationship and understanding of what needs to get accomplished matures. The reason this shift occurs is that you have accomplished the task of the half part of the model, which is designed to enable you to determine what the customer wants done, get her out of her box, and allow her to acknowledge the need for change. When this occurs, the customer is more receptive and eager to hear what you have to offer.

However, if you did not accomplish the task of creating a dialogue, getting the customer out of the box, and gathering new information, it is recommended that you not move to the last quarter of the model. By doing so, you are losing control of the call, the sale, and the relationship. It is okay to move a brief visit to the last quarter by highlighting a particular feature (character-

istic of your product or service), but you need to transition back
to the half part of the model with a good question.

## Overview

As a visual model, the quarter/half/quarter model is an ideal way
to visualize a sales call. If the customer happens to have a clock
in the office, you can very discreetly peek at the clock to time
yourself during the call. This may not be reality, but your "gut"
can be your guide when it comes to leaving one section of the
model and entering into the next. The quarter/half/quarter
model is designed for flexibility. If you are getting a sense that
you did not spend enough time in a particular section, it is okay
to go back to the section later in your sales call or conversation.
If you feel you are getting pushed too quickly out of the half part
of the model and ushered into the last quarter, transition back
to the half section in a matter of several minutes. Getting back
to one of the three sections to complete the tasks of each section
is important.

Transitions will play a key role in moving seamlessly from
one section of the model to another. As mentioned earlier in the
book, transitions are the grease that allows you to smoothly
switch from one section to another during your call. An example of this may be when a customer says to you, "I know we
scheduled an appointment to meet today, but a couple of things
have changed with my schedule. I only have a couple of minutes.
What do you have for me?" In this case, the customer is driving
you to the last quarter. She wants you to give a quick presentation. When a customer gets a quick presentation, there is a good
chance that it will not be enough to move the relationship to the
next step and will generate a false acceptance or level of interest.

In this scenario, the customer is cutting out the first two sections of the model—the opener and the half. She is requesting that you go to the last quarter. She wants you to get to the point. When this occurs, what should you do? "Should I oblige or ignore the customer and stick to my plan?" The answer of course is, it depends. This is not a good answer; however, when I was completing my graduate degree, it seemed to be an answer I received from a number of my professors when I asked a complicated question. I did not like getting that answer, nor do I like giving it to you.

When I first introduced this model several years ago, I used a more formal approach to opening the call. I had as many as five steps for the opener: introduction, gain common ground on a business level, state the reason for the call, gain customer interest, and state the objective of the meeting. All of this is good stuff, and you can use it if you like. Today, I open calls with a brief introduction of myself (if needed) and share with the customer that I would like to start the meeting or conversation with a few questions to begin the discovery process. I will tell him that I would like to run a couple of questions by him. If it is appropriate, I go on to say, "I will tell you a little bit about what my firm does, and if some of the things I mention are of interest to you, we can move forward in determining some next steps." I share with the customer that this is my plan for our conversation and ask if that sounds reasonable. In addition, I may ask how we are on time to get a sense of the "customer's clock." If he responds with a yes to my asking whether the plan sounds reasonable, I will ask if he would like to add anything additional to today's conversation. Most of the time, customers are fine with this, which actually raises a slight red flag with me as to whether they are really listening. Sometimes, before we start, the customer will ask me to tell him about my firm and what I do. When this occurs, we now know, I am being asked to shift from the opener to the last quarter. We know this will not work in our favor. When this occurs, remember to be patient with your customer. If the customer is hurrying you to the last quarter, you have to manage the situation by delivering a quick bullet point about what you do and transition back to the half part of the model. If the half part is not completed, the last quarter will lack punch and may miss the mark. Therefore, make every effort to stay on task.

## Who Has Control?

Initially, customers want control of the sales call. They have many veiled and disguised ways of getting control. The most common is their expression of interest. An example of this is when the customer opens the call for you. It could be something as innocent as, "So, what do you have new for me today?" or something a little bit more masked, such as, "Hey, I just wanted to tell you things are working great with your product, but I'm a bit short on time today. What's new?" Or, "I have a question for you. How does this work again?"

If we take the cynical approach to selling and map out what the customer is requesting using the quarter/half/quarter model, you will notice in every one of the examples, the customer is taking you from the first quarter, or opener, to the last quarter. She is expressing interest and encouraging you to tell her more about your product or service. This allows the customer to gain control of the call. If you step back for a moment, the customer is getting you to void the half part. She is shifting you directly to the last quarter. Earlier, it was mentioned that the half is one of the most crucial steps in selling. This is where it all happens. This is the section in which you achieve your edge. And the savvy customer gets you to give that all away. You are not dictating the call; the customer is. Your job is to realize it is happening and guide the conversation back to where you want it to be.

At the beginning of the call, it appears that the customer is interested in what you have to say. However, if he is just trying to get through the day, he will do his best to get you to the last quarter. Common statements that you will hear from this type of customer include:

1. What's new?
2. I am short on time, what do you have for me today?
3. I have to tell, you, you made a great presentation. I really enjoyed it. Is there anything else I should know?
4. Everything is going well with the product or service.
5. When the next opportunity arises, I will give you strong consideration and will contact you.

## Masking the Conspiracy Theory of Selling

Most customers do not like to be the bearer of bad news, so they'll couch even negative news in the most positive terms or just delay telling you the bad news (and avoid your calls) in the hope that you'll go away. It's called masking, and we all do it. Masking is when a person does not reveal his or her true feelings. At the conclusion of a recent presentation I made to a major automotive manufacturer, I was escorted to the lobby by the company's vice president of training who had chaired the meeting. He told me, "That was probably the most outstanding presentation I've ever seen." And at that moment I felt that I had lost the deal. Even though his comment was very positive, he nevertheless remained very noncommittal. If he felt that my presentation was really that good, he would have suggested further action such as, "I'm going to send you a contract," or, "I'll recommend you to my directors," or, "Here's what I want you to do." Be aware of these situations.

However, you may wonder whether the company's vice president for training simply meant what he said, that the presentation was great. Or you think that I am being skeptical. You would be correct. I am very skeptical. It enables me to make sure that I am covering all of my bases and moving at a proper pace. Let's get back to this automotive executive. Did he have a hidden agenda? In this particular case, yes. I did not get the contract. Sometimes people make simple statements that must be accepted at face value. And that's fine—in your personal life.

## Does It Happen to You?

I have enjoyed Indy car and open-wheel racing since I was a child. Growing up in Chicago gave my family easy access to the Indianapolis Motor Speedway. Each year, my family made the pilgrimage during the month of May to the track for time trials on the weekend and the big race on Memorial Day: the Indianapolis 500. To this day, I try to attend a race every now and then with my son. When I share this information with people, they look at me and say, "How can you sit there for hours and watch cars go around and around in circles?" Well, my answer is, "I can!"

Here's a story about when I was dating my wife. I suggested once that we go to an upcoming Indy car event not far from our home. Even though that conversation was many years ago, I still remember her response, "That sounds good. I'm really interested in going. Why don't you get all the details." We've been married for a long time now. I still ask her about going to the races, and she still says, "That sounds good. I'm really interested. Why don't you get all the details." After many years of marriage, I've learned that "sounds good" doesn't mean go out and get tickets. Rather it means let me know the date and I'll schedule something else for us to do.

Making this discovery in my personal life only cost me the price of two admission tickets some years ago to a race. But making the same mistake in a business situation could cost you a deal. It's very easy to misinterpret, "Sounds good. Who else is using your product or service?" It's not just a matter of hearing what you want to hear, and by that I mean you *listen* to an essentially noncommittal comment, but you *hear* a very positive statement. There's also the problem that most customers seem willing to keep the door open for the rare occasion that you might be able to help them in the future.

Instead of the customer simply saying to you, "No, no. A thousand times, no!" (or words to that effect), he misrepresents, using a variation on one of the following:

1. Sounds good.
2. Let's talk about your idea next week.
3. What's new?
4. I'm short on time. What do you have for me today?
5. I have to tell you, you made a great presentation, I really enjoyed it. Is there anything else I should know?

6. Everything makes sense with your product or service, so when the opportunity arises I will consider.
7. Is it possible that I could talk with someone who already is using your product or service?
8. Remind me again about your product.
9. Who else is using your product or service?

## Categorizing

How you manage the customer's comments, statements, or questions and even the accompanying body language will determine your ability to move the customer relationship forward. Essentially any of your customers' or prospective customers' comments, statements, or questions could be placed in one of the three following categories:

1. *Negative:* Indicates complete disinterest, skepticism, and/or resistance.
2. *Noncommittal:* Suggests an impartial attitude toward your product, idea, service, or solution.
3. *Positive*: Displays a supportive, encouraging, or optimistic position where intent of action is present.

Think about and recall some of the more common verbal and physical responses you get from customers. Using the definitions of interest listed above, which of these categories would be the most appropriate for you to place the customer's comments, statements, or questions?

Consider a common question a customer may ask, such as, "What's your product availability?" At first glance, this seems positive. You may very well think it's a step forward in your relationship with the customer, virtually a commitment. But of course it isn't, because as soon as you leave, the prospect is as likely to ask that same question to everyone he interviews that day. He may even call his current vendor to find out about product availability just to compare. Therefore, there might be just a minimal interest in your product or service.

## Be More Efficient

One of your responsibilities in managing a territory is to determine the interest level and viability of a customer. There are just so many hours in a working day. If you're going to spend them most productively, it means concentrating on your best opportunities. Ideally, then, not only do you have to categorize a prospect's level of commitment, but you also should be able to determine his or her receptiveness to change.

But what if you have only a couple of minutes to talk with your customer? If that is the case, the time segments in each component of the model get reduced dramatically. The model suggests that a nominal amount of time be spent on the opener and that more time be spent focused on the half, the part of the model that makes the difference. Remember this is the section where you gain an edge over the competition. It is okay to briefly check in with your customer, especially if you have an established relationship. However, that is not the main emphasis of the call.

Relationships are further developed by what happens in the half part of the model. Use your time utilizing what is presented in Chapter 5 on asking questions. If you happen to have more time, spread it out wisely. The real work gets done in the half part of the model. The more time you can devote to this section, the better your chance of connecting with the customer. The quarter/half/quarter model will give you balance and direction.

## It Can Happen to You

This can happen to you in a sales call. Whether you have an appointment to see a customer, a scheduled conference call, or you are doing your rounds and are just dropping in to see the customer for a few moments, the following can take place. The customer sees you and gives you a cordial greeting. You and the customer catch up on each other. Once that is complete, the customer looks you in the eyes and says, "I know we have scheduled time to speak today, but all heck is breaking loose. What do you have for me today?" Sound familiar? Maybe it is not those exact same words. Maybe the customer greets you and says, "I am short-staffed today. What's new with you?" If this has happened to you, you get the sense that the customer wants you to move things along. She wants you to get to the point. After all, it is reasonable, because she wants to stay on track and keep her day running smoothly.

Is this a customer who just wants to get through her day? In the earlier chapters, we heard from customers in the industry who are inundated with calls and requests. The more the customer can get these people to "show up and throw up," the better off he is and the better he manages his day. This is not to say that all customers are just trying to get through the day, but it does give an indication that many of them are swamped and want to move things along.

If this happens on an infrequent basis with your customer, it may be an anomaly, and you can chalk up the call to bad timing. You can make up for it the next time around. However, if this is a pattern with this customer or the industry she is in, there is a need to reassess and take control. If you enter the last quarter too soon, you are doing yourself a disservice. The problem with getting to the last quarter too early is that your solution and close will be viewed just like everyone else's. You will hear the customer say, "I am interested when the appropriate situation presents itself." In all reality, what the customer is saying is, "It's not going to happen, and I'm just being polite."

## 9

# Create a Sales Closing "Map"—A GPS to Gaining Commitment

The concepts presented in this chapter provide a strategy and tactical plan for converting a nonuser of your product or services into a loyalist. This chapter introduces "the sales map" and teaches sales professionals to design a road map for closing; to understand where the customer is on the adoption continuum; and how to shorten the sales cycle.

## Road Trip

Let's say that you decide to take the family on a vacation. The kids are out of school, and you and your spouse need a little rest and recuperation. You and the family decide to take a road trip, the classic Griswold family vacation, but this time, instead of visiting Wallyworld, you select Hollywood as your destination (if you are from the East Coast) or the Big Apple (if you are from the West Coast).

Everyone in the family is excited about the location of this year's vacation. You provide the children with a list to ensure that they bring the appropriate type and amount of clothes to avoid last-minute emergencies: shorts, sneakers, swimsuit, sun screen, wake boards, and flip-flops (New York has beaches too). You stopped the mail, turned off the water to prevent an unexpected flood in the basement, and told your neighbors to watch the place. You booked the hotel online and even made a few reservations at a couple of restaurants that were recommended to you. You pack the car and everyone is given instructions about bio-breaks. You are all set, right? You pull out of the driveway and start heading to your destination.

You planned everything for your trip, but you didn't map out the route. You decided to leave that up to chance. You made the decision to just start driving west or east, depending on your destination. You didn't get a map, and you don't own a global positioning system (GPS). You didn't even access MapQuest for directions. Undaunted, you start driving. You elect to go by instinct, maybe use a compass to point you in the right direction or allow the stars to be your guide. You find the nearest road and start driving in what you believe is the right direction. It is possible that you will get to your final destination, after many trials and tribulations. It might take you too much time, and others taking the same trip, who have a solid sense of direction and a map, will pass you along the way. If you are lucky, you might make it at least halfway, maybe to the Mississippi River. Not bad, you got to see the Gateway Arch in St. Louis instead of the Empire State Building or catching a wave in La Jolla. You got halfway, but you didn't get to your final destination.

## Selling Is Like Planning for a Vacation

In sales, just like in vacation planning, you probably will not arrive at your final destination if you don't plan out the details and know how you are going to get there. If you think about it, you probably have a number of customers around the Mississippi River. They are buying from you. They are selecting your product or service. But you know that they could and should be buying more. Every person reading this book has driven a couple of customers all the way to the opposite coast. Was it luck, a good sense of direction, or a combination of both? Whatever the answer, I am guessing that everyone reading this book has a handful or a growing number of customers who are sitting stuck around the Mississippi River. They are purchasing or selecting your product or service, but they have not decided to make what you offer a "universal fit" for their practice, department, operation, business, or company.

## Create the Map, and They Will Come

If you have a map that tells you what to do for every call, you know where you are and where you need to be. It can be that simple. Create the map, and they will come. That is what is introduced to you over the next several chapters: how to create a GPS for closing. In this chapter, we introduce the concepts of creating a map and the four customer segments.

The key to a good trip is to get there as soon and as well as possible. You want to eliminate the possibility of getting lost and minimize the possibility of delay. As you chart your course, you want to be able to receive constant updates about the road conditions. Are there any accidents, road closures, or issues with weather? With any trip, short or long, it is helpful to know if there is a problem on your route. The driving force of creating a sales map is to put you and your customers on the Autobahn for moving your existing relationships forward to the next level.

## Taking the Trip

To illustrate my point, I would like to share with you a story about a trip I took with my family. A number of years ago my family and I decided to visit a property in West Virginia called the Greenbrier Resort, a beautiful location in a remote part of the state. About two weeks prior to the trip, my wife asked me if I knew how to get there. With some hesitation, I sheepishly admitted that I did not. She told me that we had just renewed our membership in AAA, and she would stop by to pick up a map at one of its nearby locations. A day later, I left to go out of town to conduct a series of seminars and keynotes, and I arrived home late in the evening several days later. As I entered my kitchen area and turned on the light, I noticed a booklet on the counter. To the best of my recollection, it was a six-by-eight inch spiral-bound booklet. When I opened it up, I saw that the left-hand side pocket contained a map. Curious, I opened the map. There in front of me was my route to the Greenbrier Resort. The entire route was highlighted with a yellow marker. I thought to myself, this is nice. My route is completely illustrated to me from start to finish. But that was not all; the booklet also contained a computer printout telling me the routes, exact mileage, and estimated duration of time on each thoroughfare. This was awesome. This booklet told me where I needed to be at all times and how long it would take me to get where I needed to be. In addition, it provided suggestions for handling any problems that might arise. I learned that this booklet is called a TripTik. That is what this chapter provides: a GPS to closing, a TripTik to get your customer to the final destination—being an advocate of your product or service.

## How to Create the Map

Let's put some things into perspective. A number of years ago the New York Sales and Marketing Club (NYSMC) commissioned a survey to find out the number of steps it takes to close a sale. Its conclusion was that 81 percent of the time, business is closed on the fifth step. The steps the NYSMC identified were:

Step 1. Introduction
Step 2. Meet additional decision makers
Step 3. Make a presentation
Step 4. Submit a proposal
Step 5. Close

These five steps could be considered fairly standard for most industries but not all that applicable to others.

This number of steps may be higher or lower than what you have experienced with the sale of your product or service. What the New York Sales and Marketing Club did not identify was the actual number of contacts (sales and phone calls) it took in each step to be successful.

During a typical day or week in your territory, you make every effort to advance the sales process. The New York Sales and Marketing Club suggests that it takes five steps to close. The key to becoming more effective is to reduce the number of contacts in accomplishing each step. For example, you have three appointments one morning. At the end of the first call, you start to wrap up by believing that the call appeared to go well. The discussion and presentation portion seemed meaningful. You ask the prospective customer to allow you to come back and meet with other individuals involved in the decision-making process. After brief consideration, the prospective customer agrees. The customer says that this would be a good idea. You are on target with this company, meaning that after one contact, you are moving to the next step in the sales cycle.

Let's now move to the next appointment you have that day. Everything appears to go well. At the end of the call, you ask the prospective customer to allow you to schedule another visit and to include anyone else involved in the process. After a moment of contemplating, the prospective customer responds by saying, "I am not ready for that right now. Why don't you come back and meet with me again?" The door is still open, and the prospective customer is still interested; however, you were unsuccessful in moving to the next step. The steps have not changed, but now the number of contacts to move through the steps successfully has expanded.

Let's look at the third call that is scheduled for the morning. This call also appears to be going well. After about 15 minutes with the prospective customer, he stops the meeting and suggests that the discussion has been well received and that he would like to have his department head join the meeting. In this case, an additional decision maker has entered the picture on the first contact. In this scenario, the steps have not changed, but the number of contacts to move through the steps has been reduced. The goal of creating a sales map, along with the content of the preceding chapters, is to allow you to reduce the number of contacts to move a prospective nonuser customer of your product or service to advocate status. The goal is to shorten and make the sales process more effective. Reducing the number of contacts and the amount of time it takes to drive the customer to his or her final destination—advocacy status—will make you more productive. You will be able to accomplish more in less time.

## Do Not Rush the Process

Here's another analogy. Many of you have experienced the dating cycle, which has parallels to the sales cycle. For the most part, just like in any relationship that you want to last a long time, you don't want to rush into the relationship. On the other hand, you don't want things to take too long. Since the majority of people are familiar with this topic, it makes for a good analogy for the validation of the sales cycle you are about to design. When you meet a person for the first time and you both decide to see each other on a date, a popular first-date destination is a lunch meeting. Lunch has a lot of advantages. It's short, so if it isn't going well, you always have an excuse to leave, especially during the work week. You can arrive separately, so you don't have to rely on each other for transportation, and you can come and go as you please. Another advantage is that a restaurant is a public place, so there is safety in being out in the open, and it's affordable for whoever is paying.

So step 1 in the dating cycle is lunch. Let's say that the lunch goes well. Probably the next step is to try to spend more time with each other, something like dinner and a movie. Therefore, step 2 is dinner. Dinner gives you an opportunity to get to know each other a little better and the show or movie takes the pressure off of having to converse with one another for several hours straight. And, at the end of the show, it gives you something to talk about over coffee. If that evening goes well, then step 3 in your dating cycle is probably spending an afternoon together. This date could be going to a museum, the beach, a lake, a ball game, skiing, a concert, an event, and so on. In this step, the time commitment is advanced rather dramatically, because this step will probably take up a good bit of the afternoon and maybe part of the night. During this step, friends may also be introduced. If this step goes well and several of the prior steps are repeated, there is a good chance that the relationship will move forward. In moving toward step 4, there is a strong probability that this is where the relationship will take a major advancement. This is the step where you might meet family members or go to a family function or a day trip. Keep in mind that if you introduce family members too soon, it may jeopardize the relationship. The other person may feel that things are being too rushed. If step 4 occurs, you can transition easily to step 5, which is defined as becoming "involved" in a serious relationship. Once you reach step 5, things could be pretty well on the way.

Let's compare the sales and dating cycle. Selling is somewhat like dating. If the process is pushed forward too quickly, failure is probable. For example, if you went from step 1 directly to steps 4 or 5, I think you'll agree the process would break down because you are moving too fast. This also applies to the dating process. Does it make sense to go from the step 1 lunch directly to meeting the family? Chances are you are moving too fast, and that is not what the other person had signed up for. No need to meet Mom on the second date! And of course, how would you respond if the person that just met you suggests after lunch that the first date went so well that they would like to get involved in a serious relationship? If you heard that request, I bet you would be running for the door! That is also true in selling.

By now you are getting the picture. What applies to the dating process also applies to selling. If you don't map out the process or if you move too fast, it breaks down. But taking the opposite tactic could be just as damaging. If you wait too long to move the process forward, other players may get into the picture, the interest level may wane, and you might not have the chance to change a customer's schema and alter her purchasing or selection habits.

## Get the Picture?

To be more successful and efficient, it is important to determine the number of steps in your cycle and create a map that takes the customer from the beginning to the end. Creating this map will enable you to check your progress in moving the business relationship forward (to the next step). Creating a map that contains steps enables you to know where you are and how to check your progress. It keeps you on track and will enable you to know exactly where the customer is on the map and where you have to take her. Knowing where you want to go makes it much easier for you to gain commitment.

## How Many Contacts to Get to Your Final Destination?

For years my firm was involved in the performance assessment of many sales forces. We looked at each industry to determine the average number of contacts (sales/phone calls) it takes to change a nonuser of a product or service to an advocate. As you can imagine, the numbers varied a bit. Overall, we did conclude that the average number of contacts it takes to start and finish your trip appears to be 20. It will take 20 contacts to move the customer along the continuum to advocate status. The number 20 can be an initial guide for you. Your industry and the product or services you provide may require an adjustment to this number. Some of you reading this book will need to complete the process in a shorter time frame, while other sales scenarios may take many years. Once you determine the average number of contacts you need, you can create your map. The next step is to identify your customer segments.

## Segmenting Your Customer

Once you have determined the number of contacts it will take you to move a nonuser of your product or service to an advocate, the next step is to determine how many customer segments you will need. Typically, there are four customer segments. They are nonuser, light user, moderate user, and advocate. Four segments seem to be a good number to help organize your customer base. On occasion, I have worked with companies that have five, six, or seven segments. The more segments you have, the more difficult it will be to determine where your customer fits on your map.

### Mapping It Out in Segments

Your map should start with four segments of customers: the nonuser, light user, moderate user, and advocate. Identifying these four segments allows you to determine where each of your customers is located. For example, a nonuser is stuck on one of the coasts. An advocate or loyalist is in your destination city (Los Angeles or New York). The light user is somewhere near the Mississippi River, and the moderate user is halfway between the coast and the center of the country.

## Nonuser Prospective Customer

For the most part, this is a loose interpretation that you can tailor as you evolve with your map. The first segment, the nonuser, is pretty clear-cut—this is a prospective customer who does not use your product or service. Currently she is satisfied with another vendor's product or service. This is a customer who has placed little or no value on your product or service and does not view your product or service as a better solution for her current application or needs. This customer's mental framework as defined by her schema does not support what you are selling. The nonuser prospective customer is essentially a "nonbeliever" in your product or service. The focus on closing these customers is to get them educated about what you have to offer. Trying to get this customer segment to purchase or select your product or service will have limited success. This customer will not move forward or consider your solution until her schema has been altered and you have educated her as to why there is a need for change. Closing this segment of customer without the proper education and the breaking of her selection process will result in a false acceptance. A false acceptance is when a customer tells you what you want to hear to get you out of her office with little or no progress in moving the relationship forward.

## Light User

The second customer segment is a light user. The goal with this customer segment is to get him to start to use or purchase your product or service. Access to this segment depends upon your ability to find an opportunity for him to use what you are selling. Therefore, getting the customer to start to use your product is the overriding objective in this segment. This customer is a person, department, or company that has knowledge of your product or service but is not completely aware of all of the features and benefits your product or service can offer. For this reason, ongoing and continued education about your product is required. In addition, you need to promote out-of-the-box thinking and discussion to give yourself a chance of finding a place where the prospective customer could use your product or service. If this customer identifies an area to use your product or service, it will most likely occur because he has uncovered or recognized an appropriate "niche" for what you are selling. Possibly the niche would be a failure or disappointment in his current vendor's ability to provide a solution in a particular application or situation. Therefore, it is important to identify a niche to start the purchasing of your product or service and the continuation of the education process.

## Moderate User

Once you have a department, person, or company using your product or service, the next step is to make the customer use it more. You want her to become a moderate user, the customer segment in which you target expansion of the application of your product or service. This expansion can take several forms. The first can be the use of your current product or service in other departments or areas of the company. The other way to expand business is to have the customer use different products or services that are not currently being used. Taking the light user to a moderate is the segment in which you will probably spend the most time. Historically, most salespeople have about 50 percent of their customer base in the light user segment. The key to success is moving as many light users to moderate as possible. This seems to be a reasonable statement, but it can be a difficult task. The light user, however, is using your product for only a select number of her applications or needs. The balance of her product selection is going to someone you compete with. If you can get a light user to expand her use for your product or service, this customer segment could pay the biggest reward. A moderate user customer is a customer who has participated in most of the educational activities and provided access and has used your product or service for certain applications or situations. Predominantly, this customer sees value in your product or service but has not identified it as a "universal" solution for all her applications and/or departments. Therefore, it is important to continue to expand on the existing user and identify a new area for application. Moving the light to the moderate will probably become your biggest focus because of the large numbers of light users you have in your territory.

## The Advocate

The final customer segment category is the advocate or loyalist. This is the customer who uses your product or service exclusively. This is the customer you need to protect so that you don't lose business. An advocate customer is a customer who has participated in all the educational activities, provided access, and is using your product or service for most applications and departments. For the most part, this customer sees tremendous value in your product or service and is a true supporter.

Now that you know there are four customer segments, you need to place each of your customers into one of the four categories. Once you place the customer into the segment, you need to move him or her to the next segment and constantly monitor the progression.

## Closing Each Segment

You have been introduced to the four segment types. I suggest that your map contain approximately 20 contacts to get you started. Breaking the numbers down gives each segment five closes. Crafting five closes for each segment will allow you to move the relationship forward. It will give you five different options per category to gain commitment. If one series of requests or closes does not work, you can apply up to four more for each category. Including a minimum of five closes per segment allows you to measure your progression in the relationship. If the customer is compliant and agrees to your requests to close, you know you are moving forward. You are moving closer to your final destination. To gain commitment from most contacts, I would like to share with you a very powerful concept in the next chapter, one that I have evolved over the years.

# 10

# Reciprocal
# Consideration

To enable you to gain commitment on most contacts and to move your customer from a nonuser to an advocate, I would like to introduce you to a concept called *reciprocal consideration.*

Reciprocal consideration (RC) originally was authored by Robert Cialdini, then a professor at Arizona State University, who introduced the concept in his book, *Influence: The Psychology of Persuasion* (revised edition, William Morrow, 1993). In his book, Cialdini discusses a series of empirical studies he conducted on how to influence and persuade individuals. It is a very interesting read.

Imagine this: A Boy Scout in full uniform rings your doorbell. When you answer the door, he politely introduces himself to you and explains that his Boy Scout troop is having a dinner dance at the local firehouse hall the following night (Saturday night). He describes the evening and asks you to purchase a ticket for you and another guest for $150. Put yourself in that position.

How would you react? You are given very short notice. You process the possibility of spending $150 for a dinner dance at a local firehouse.

You look at the young lad on your stoop. You don't want to be rude, but you don't want to spend $150 at a function you know nothing about. Upon hearing his request, you graciously decline his offer and tell him it would not be convenient for you to attend. You tell the boy that it sounds like a great event, but unfortunately you have plans for the evening. At that moment you don't feel great about delivering the news, but on the other hand you are not going to attend his function, whether you were actually busy or not. Case closed right? Nope.

Hearing your refusal, the Boy Scout acknowledges that $150 is a lot of money and it is short notice to attend the function. But before leaving, he asks one more question. "I understand you might not want to spend $150 to attend the dinner dance, but would you buy a one-dollar candy bar to support our troop?" Bingo! You got closed for a buck. Rumor has it that the Boy Scout knocked on approximately a hundred doors and collected $100.

The concept of reciprocal consideration is powerful. It serves up two requests that will generate a yes *and* a no. The difference between Professor Cialdini's research and your real-world selling scenario is that both of your requests need to be viewed as reasonable. The Boy Scout story suggests that the first request was unreasonable and that the second was very acceptable. If you can pair two reasonable requests that align with the segment of your customer, your success rate should be very good. Using RC appropriately will generate a yes-no answer 65 percent of the time; yes-yes 15 percent of the time; and no-no 20 percent of the time it is applied. This suggests that your close could be successful up to 80 percent of the time it is employed.

The concept of reciprocal consideration is powerful. It serves up two realistic requests that will generate a yes and a no answer 65 to 80 percent of the time it is applied. What is interesting is when the customer says no, he feels he has won, but he gets to say yes to one of your requests. And you win because it is one of the steps on your map.

To give you an idea of how this works, I would like to share with you how my son unknowingly used this on me. I am guessing that if you are a parent, you may have a couple of rules that need to be followed when your children are at home. Some of the rules are centered on behavior and some of them around other issues. One of the rules that we have at the house is that we like to limit the amount of junk food or sweets consumed during the week. We try to maintain a healthy lifestyle that consists of exercise and good food choices. Not too long ago, we had a birthday party for my youngest child. The party was held over the weekend. After the party there was plenty of leftover cake sitting in our refrigerator. One night during the week, my son came barreling down the steps and said to me: "Dad, can I have a piece of cake and two cookies?" I responded by saying: "No, you can have a cookie." After I told him that he could only have a cookie, I realized what had just happened. If he had asked for a piece of cake, I would have said no. If he had asked for a cookie, I would have said no. But the combination of two separate requests got him the result he wanted. I hope to get you the results you want.

The application of reciprocal consideration fits perfectly with what this book has suggested—moving the relationship to the next step. By positioning your close in this manner, you have positioned yourself for success. By gaining commitment to one of the two requests, you are able to move to the next city on your map. And you win, because you have gotten the customer to do something that indicates interest in advancing the relationship.

The dual requests of the RC close are used to compel the customer to comply with one of the two choices you provided. Using this closing format enables you to gain traction with the customer. It will help you to identify whether the customer is willing to do one of the two items you requested. If she selects one of the two items, she is indicating her willingness to advance the consultative relationship. The key to making this work for you is the combination of requests and the delivery of the requests, which will be based on where you are on the map.

## Combination of Requests

Selecting your combination of requests will depend on where your customer is on the map. Is he a nonuser, light user, moderate user, or advocate? Once you know where the customer is, the RC close should be designed to get you to the next segment. For example, if you are calling on a light user, you want to move the customer to a moderate stance. On the other hand, if you are calling on a nonuser, you want the customer to start using your product or service. If you are just starting out and establishing the relationship, the combination of requests is somewhat easier to comply with, compared to the end of the road, where the requests are more demanding.

During the development of this technique, a number of business professionals were polled to determine what motivated them to consider a different product or service from the one they were then using. Of those people who responded, an overwhelming number gave one of two answers: They will make a change to another product because they think it will be better than what they are using now, or they would make a selection because they felt it would be better to change. Where the first group used logic to make a decision, the second group used their heart, or emotions.

Because of these responses, the RC close is crafted to capture both the logic/head and the emotion/heart of the customer. The first request should be focused around the head of the customer, and the second request should target his or her emotions. This combination provides a powerful motivator to get the customer to reconsider his or her current position and become disposed to moving the relationship forward.

The key to making this skill work for you is the combination of appropriate requests. If you are in the early stage of the relationship, consider focusing your requests on tasks that will educate the customer on your product or service. If you are in the middle of the trip, focus on continuing the educational process and getting the customer to demonstrate or experience the application of your product or service on a trial basis. If you are trying to make the customer a moderate user, ask the customer to continue with his current use of your product or service and expand its usage in other areas of the company or select additional products or services that you provide. If you have an advocate, keep reinforcing that he is making the right decision and that the results of using your product or service have met or exceeded his expectations.

## Know Your Requests

Part of your precall planning should include determining the two requests that you will ask for at the end of the call. Once you determine these two items, be certain that the request focuses on both the logic and emotion of the customer to gain compliance.

Every week and probably almost every day, your customers hear a couple of closing lines that they dislike. When they hear the close they tend to dislike, they often give the salesperson a false acceptance by agreeing with the request to get the salesperson out of the office or off the phone. The application of reciprocal consideration fits perfectly with the notion of developing a sales map. Reciprocal consideration is something that your customer is not familiar with and is the opposite of what the customer dislikes. By using reciprocal consideration, you are making it all about the customer and his issues. By presenting your close in this manner, you have positioned yourself for success. The RC close consists of the following three parts:

Fair to say
Reasonable
Let's do this

The first statement in the RC close that you need to deliver to the customer is, "Is it fair to say . . . ?" The second statement that needs to be delivered is, "Is it reasonable . . . ?" And the third and final statement that needs to be delivered is the actual request: "Let's do this." This format enables you to gain traction with the customer. The key to making this work is the combination of requests, which is based on what category the customer is in now: nonuser, light user, moderate user, or advocate.

During the development of this program, a number of customers were polled to determine what motivated them to try a different product. The two common answers that I shared with you earlier were a decision based on head or logic and a decision using heart or emotions. The second group of customers suggested that they make a decision using their heart or emotions. Because of this answer, the "fair to say" is built around the "head" of the customer and the "reasonable" is aimed at targeting the "heart" of the customer. This combination provides a powerful motivator to get the customer to reconsider his current purchasing habits and product or service selections. The role of "fair to say" and "reasonable" is to set up and validate your actual closing request. These two elements assist your efforts to get the customer to do something different. "Fair to say" and "reasonable" connect with the day-to-day experiences of the customer. This connection leads to agreement from the customer and makes your closing requests practical.

## Guiding Principles

To properly apply the RC close, you need to adhere to the following guiding principles:

1.  Each request must be different and not contingent on the other. For example, you can't ask a customer to read an article and then ask to come back to talk to her about it. The RC close needs to contain two distinct, clear, and separate items.
2.  Avoid words like *always, a lot,* and *many* and replace them with words like *some, a couple,* and *a few*. Omit concrete words that tend to create barriers with customers. They suggest that what they are doing all the time is not correct. By using words like, some, a few, or a couple, you can gain greater traction and credibility and get the customer to comply with your request. Using these words eliminates the notion of fault.
3.  Use action words that denote a request. These words could be: *switch, select, start,* or *try*. This is a polite request for action

and not consideration. Using these words and other similar
ones makes it very clear to the customer what you are asking. You are making a request for her to follow through and
complete.

4.  Make sure you use the word *and*, not *or*, in combining the
    request. This triggers the yes/no response. If my son asked
    me for a piece of cake or a cookie, the answer would have
    been different. Keep thinking "cake and cookie" when you
    go for the close!

## Targeting the Close

Crafting an appropriate and effective close will require some
homework. Talk with the support personnel that assist your customer in his day-to-day activities. If you can get access to these
individuals, ask them some questions. Find out the issues and
problems that the customer is struggling with, what keeps him
up at night. Research the customer's company and industry. Discover the inherent issues and challenges that your customer and
his company face that get in the way of progress. Inserting these
challenges in the RC close template will enable you to hit the
bull's-eye. If you can uncover these issues, your close will be on
point. The more specific and pertinent the "fair to say" and "reasonable" statements are, the greater the likelihood of your receiving a yes-yes answer to your close. The purpose of the "fair to
say" and "reasonable" statements is to avoid allowing the customer to say no. If he says no to both requests, the trip to the
next city has stopped. Your car has broken down. You are in need
of roadside assistance.

# 11

# Dealing with Customer Put-Offs

## When Customers Indicate Interest

Turning a prospective customer into an actual customer can be difficult. Most days you may meet with negative comments and a lack of interest for your product or service. Customers may voice their level of satisfaction with their current vendors and tell you that they will keep you in mind. However, on occasion there is a possibility that a prospective customer will indicate interest in what you have to say or offer. The following questions and statements may indicate interest:

1. Who else is using your product or service?
2. Do you have some articles or surveys for me to review?
3. I like what I am hearing, but the next step would be for me to bring this to the selection committee.

4.  Let me talk with my partners.
5.  Just remind me again about your product the next time I see you.
6.  Are you an approved vendor?
7.  Where has your product or service worked?
8.  What is your success rate or return on investment (ROI)?

When you hear comments or questions like these from a prospective customer, you may get excited. Your inner voice says to you, "I just received a buying signal. Finally, someone is interested in what I have to say!" It is more than likely that this has happened to you. So what do you do? Let's role-play how this conversation with a customer might sound.

## Customer Comments

You may have heard your customer say: "What you are saying is interesting, but I would like to see a study or report." And when you hear that, how do you respond? When a customer says he needs to see a study, the standard response might be, "Yes, I have a great article about the performance of our product. The article talks about how well our product performed in a very difficult application. The article is about three pages long. Would you like a copy?" The customer will probably respond with a positive answer. The next question lobbed at the prospective customer will be something like, "Do you need anything else from me at this time?" Chances are the prospective customer will respond with something along the lines of, "No, if you could get me that article, that would be great. The article will give me a better understanding of what your product can do for me." The typical salesperson response might sound like this, "That's great. When should I get back to you?" The savvy prospective customer will say, "Why don't you give me a week or two to review the article and absorb the information?"

Sound familiar? What has just transpired is what I call *corporate protocol*. This means that the prospective customer is expecting the type of questions that you are asking, and you as the salesperson pretty much expect the responses you're getting. It is a cordial return of questions and answers. And both parties know that once this banter is complete, the sales call is over. When the dance is done, you leave the customer's office or hang up the phone pleased with your progress.

You feel excited. The prospective customer told you he was interested in more information about the performance of your product. Not only are you excited, but so is the prospective customer, but not for the reasons you would like to hear. The prospective customer is excited because he was able to blow you off for several weeks and you were happy to go. This is called futuring.

## Futuring

When a customer, prospective customer, or even an individual outside of work, indicates interest but postpones the decision, you just got "futured." Has this ever happened to you? Several weeks pass from your initial meeting with the prospective customer who requested more information about the performance of your product. You return several weeks later to meet with her to talk about the article. Anxious to hear what she has to say, you open the call by focusing on her thoughts and her perspective on what she read. Waiting for the answer, your mind swirls with positive thoughts. "Maybe this will be the prospective customer who will buy from me today." Then the bomb drops. The prospective customer looks you straight in the eye and with the most remorseful tone of voice says, "I am so sorry. Things have been hectic around here. I don't have time to breathe, let alone carve out some time to read your article." She follows up with, "I am still interested. Can you get back to me when things slow down in a few weeks?" Did you ever hear that? Of course you did. Not only did the customer blow you off once, but she is blowing you off again. I call that being doubled futured!

Let's rewind the tape and try this again.

Prospective customer: What you are saying is interesting, but I would like to see a study or report to give me more information.

Your response: Yes, I have a great article about the performance of our product. The article talks about how well our product performed in a very difficult application. The article is about three pages in length, would you like a copy?

Prospective customer: Yes, that would be great; I would be interested in reading it.

Your response: I will be glad to send it to you. Do you need anything else from me at this time?

Prospective customer: No, you have done a good job. This is more than I expected would occur. If you could get that article to me in a timely manner, that would be great. The article will give me a better understanding of what your product can do for me.

Your response: I can e-mail the article to you tomorrow and place a hard copy in the mail for you. When should I get back to you?

Prospective customer: Why don't you give me a week or two to review the article and absorb its information?

As I mentioned before, both parties know that in a matter of minutes or even seconds this sales call or conversation is over. But this is where it begins to become fun for you. Once you have recognized that you are being futured, you can implement a new approach to determine the prospective customer's true interest level.

Many people have fallen victim to the put-off called futuring. The customer seems interested. She wants to learn more about your product. But you as the salesperson might not even realize you are allowing things to get away from you. You are allowing the customer to slip away. To stop that from happening and regain control of the sales call, conversation, and relationship, you have to create the future in the present. You have to set up the customer for the right defining question.

The first thing that you need to do is realize that you are being futured. When you are getting put off to some time in the future, you need to recognize that it is happening. You need to know how to handle it. It might happen next week. A couple of days after reading this book you will probably hear a prospective customer deliver one of the statements or questions indicating interest that we mentioned earlier in this chapter. When you hear the customer voice one of these statements or comments, or others like these, you need to stop, acknowledge, and respond. Regain your composure and realize that you're being futured. Once you have realized it is happening, it could be too late to respond. That is okay. The first step in recovery is to acknowledge that it is taking place.

## Turning the Tables

Let's get back to our example in which the customer tells you that she would like to read an article. It is still recommended that you respond in the way that you always have. You can still ask the traditional questions and get the typical answers that a prospective customer will give you. However, just when the customer thinks she is getting rid of you, you turn the tables on her. This is when she least expects it.

You say to the prospective customer in a very conversational tone: "Let's say that in a couple of days from now you happen to have a few quiet moments at the office and you are sitting at your desk. You see my article and decide to pick it up. When you read the article, it will confirm most of the things that I have been saying and give strong evidence of our product's performance." You then go on to say, "When you read that information, what do you feel will happen, and how will this information affect your thought process?"

By asking this question, you have created an environment that projects the customer to the time in question. You have futured her. You have defined the prospective customer's interest in reading your article, and you are looking to determine if she is willing to move forward or not. This follow-up question and scenario allow you to get a true indication of the prospective customer's level of interest.

If the prospective customer gives you a solid answer and outlines a few steps that may occur in the upcoming weeks to further the relationship, you have determined her interest. On the other hand, if the prospective customer provides you with an abrupt, curt answer, you have discovered that the prospective customer was just trying to get rid of you.

# The Most Unexpected Answers

Futuring can generate some memorable answers. I would like to share two of these with you. In my business, we often receive requests from prospective clients to speak with our references. In our case, a reference is an existing client who has experienced and attended a live or Web-based training seminar that we provide. When the request is made for a reference, the client prefers to speak to someone in his or her own industry. Fortunately, after many years in the industry conducting thousands of programs, we can accommodate most requests.

Some time ago, two separate and identical futuring occurrences unfolded in a relatively short period of time, both resulting from requests for references. In the first example, toward the end of an initial conversation that was centered mostly on the discovery process, a prospective client asked if it would be possible for me to provide any references from his industry. As soon as I heard the request, I knew I was being futured. I replied that we had several. I went on to ask, "What would be the best way for me to send the information to you, and do you have a specific timeline?" The prospective client responded that an e-mail would be fine and to call him in about two weeks. I acknowledged his answer and said I would e-mail the information shortly. I then went on to say that I could contact him in about three weeks to allow some more time. The prospective client responded that additional time would not be necessary. I then switched from traditional mode to futuring mode. I asked, "Before we hang up, to allow me to prepare for our next conversation, could I ask you a quick question?" I wanted to transition the prospective client and put him on my agenda. He responded positively. I started by saying, "To help me prepare for the next time we talk, I want to run a scenario by you." I then said, "Since you will be calling my references, there is a strong likelihood that they will say some very positive things about our seminars. In some cases, they might even tell you that the work we did for them was one of the best seminars they ever sponsored. If you were to hear that, what do you feel is our next step to move forward?" Ah, the priceless MasterCard answer! You are probably thinking, "Wow, now that is a great question." This particular prospective client paused for a moment to gather his thoughts. He responded by saying, "If everything checks out, which I expect it would, we will move forward with a rollout of your content at our upcoming national meeting." Now that is a good answer. And, off the record, that is what actually occurred.

The second example about references took place a few days after the scenario I just described. This prospective client response, however, had a different ending. Exactly the same banter took place, as did the same setup and transition, but the ending was not what I expected. When I got futured, I repeated the same thing that I said a couple of days before to the prospective client: "To help me prepare for the next time we talk, I want to run a scenario by you. Since you will be calling my references, there is a strong likelihood that they will say some very positive things about our seminars. In some cases, they might even tell you that the work we did for them was one of the best seminars ever sponsored. If you were to hear that, what do you feel is our next step to move forward?" I delivered the perfect futuring response. I waited with baited breath, thinking that I would triumph again. You won't be able to get off the hook with me! Then something unusual occurred: I heard dead silence and a dial tone. I got hung up on!

One minute the person wants to call my references and the next I get, "If you would like to make a call, please hang up and dial again." I rushed out of my office to relay what had just happened. I told everyone the story and started laughing: "Can you believe that—he hung up on me!" So, what is the moral of the story? If you don't clarify the true interest level of clients, they will keep stringing you along. I feel it is better to know where you stand and the actual interest level of the prospective customer. Even though this was an anomaly and it happened to me only once in about 20 years, the story is nevertheless worth sharing. Why? Because if you don't realize you are being futured, the prospective client can drag you around forever, and you might forecast her as a pending sale waiting to happen.

## Keep the Customer on the Hook

One of my favorite sayings is not to allow the customer off the hook. Too often, salespeople accept the crumbs that are thrown their way. If a customer knows he can blow you off, he will. If the customer knows he can act interested and demand that you jump through hoops, he will. If you constantly jump through hoops without any commitments, the customer will put you on a pogo stick.

In any relationship, there needs to be an even balance, a set of understood expectations, and a mutual agreement to work things out. In business, those same requirements should be present. In your advocate relationships, those elements are present. There are too many prospective customers who want to walk all over you and take advantage of the resources you can provide. Sometimes we agree to those requests with very little commitment on the part of the prospective customer in hope of gaining favor. Futuring is about striking an even balance. Prospective customers do not treat their preferred vendors poorly. Futuring attempts to get you on an even playing field.

## Prioritizing

A driving force behind futuring is to help you prioritize the interest level of your prospective and existing customers. If, over the course of a month, you are futured a dozen times (this number may be high or low), futuring will help you to determine who is willing to make a decision, put in the necessary time required to investigate your solution, change his or her schemas, and select your product or service. If out of the twelve prospective customers that future you, only three or four give you a solid answer and course of action, you have just identified who wants to play ball with you. You have also identified the eight prospective customers who will just siphon up as much information from you as possible until you give up. Much like the idea of establishing a map to drive your prospective customer to the advocacy segment, the concept of futuring gives you a tool to determine the interest level of the prospective customer. The more interested and invested prospective customers you add to your day-to-day activities, the better chance you have of using your time wisely. At the beginning of my sales career I was a pit bull. I would call on prospective customers until I was blue in the face. And you know what happened—nothing! Why? Because I was not aware of what prospective customers were doing to me. They were keeping the other guy honest. They would get all my information and use it to their advantage. Rarely did I get an order in these scenarios. I expended all that effort and work for relatively nothing in return. I wish I had known about futuring when I was just starting out.

Futuring is about making you more productive in your efforts as a professional in selling. Think back to all the times that prospective customers requested information from you. Blindly you fulfilled their requests in the hope of getting an edge.

Sure, it worked sometimes, but more often it did not. It just wasted your time. Futuring will allow you to prioritize who is interested and who is not. If you are in an industry that does not allow you to dismiss prospective customers who are not responsive to your requests, at least you can put them on the bottom of your target list. By realizing that you are being futured, you can do something about it. You can make a better determination about the amount of resources and time you are willing to extend to prospective customers, based on the quality of their responses.

## Creating the Future in the Present

Managing the customer's put-off requires you to be professional, patient, and conversational. It can be frustrating to realize that you are being futured. Handling the situation improperly can cause you more frustration. By using the concepts in this chapter, you can move some of your futuring relationships forward. By responding to the customer's futuring statement with a "creating a future in the present" response, you are building credibility. The customer will realize that you cannot be bullied. She will respect you for the way you handle the situation.

### Recognizing Futuring

The first important thing for you to know is whether futuring is occurring. To help you recognize the situation, list on a sheet of paper all the statements you hear during the normal course of a day, week, and month. Write down all the statements customers make to you that indicate interest. Determine which ones put you off into sometime in the future. Obvious futuring statements are the ones where the customer says, "Call me next quarter; we don't have a budget this year." "Call me in the fall when we start the budgeting process." "Our current contract is not up for another 12 months." These comments and others like them are clear indications that you are being futured.

When you are futured, it does not mean that the customer is lying and just trying to get rid of you. It could be very true that there is no money in the budget or the existing supplier has the business locked up for a year. But it is important for you to determine where things will stand when the contract is up and new budget money is available.

The not-so-obvious futuring statements are a little more difficult to detect. They could be masked. They may include the following:

1. I use your product as much as I can when the situation arises.
2. Remind me again where it is best to use your product or service.
3. Can you talk with my design person?
4. I like what I am hearing; we just do not have an immediate application now.
5. Who else is using your solution?
6. When the time comes, I will reevaluate your services.

These statements and others might be a little more difficult to identify. Once you identify that you are being futured, the battle is half over. The next part of the battle is to handle it correctly.

## Understanding the Future Event

The next important element is to understand the future event—what will happen when the time in question occurs? For example, if the customer tells you to contact him at the end of the year when the new budgeting process for the next year starts, your job is to determine the level of interest from the prospective customer when the time in question occurs. In this scenario, it is at the end of the year. It is clear that you are being put off until November or December. The customer is indicating a willingness to talk at that time; however, he is shutting the door on you now and not allowing it to open until November or December comes around. In the interim, opportunities can be lost. The cornerstone of futuring is to understand what will happen when the future event occurs. If you were to actually receive a response like this, you would say: "Let's say it is at the end of the year. It is starting to get a little cold, and you finally have your budget numbers approved. Can you share with me how you would go about determining if our service is the one that you might select over your other choices?" By asking this question and creating the future in the present, you have eliminated the resistance that the prospective customer has raised. You are erasing that issue and peeling back the customer's veneer to determine his true interest level.

Another example of futuring is when the customer asks if you have documentation to validate what you are saying. Asking for validation is a reasonable request from the customer. Here is a possible response, "If you were to have a couple of minutes in the next few days and you read my information, chances are that it will confirm some of the things that I have been saying. What do you feel will happen next?" Crafting this type of response will give you an understanding of where the customer is positioned. Like the game of poker, you need to know the strength of your hand. The same thing is true with futuring. By asking the customer what will happen once he reads the documentation, you can get a sense of where you are positioned. The customer will give you an indication of whether he intends to move forward. The same is true with the prior example about the year-end budget. Projecting out to the future enables you to have a discussion with the customer as if the event actually had occurred. It is incumbent upon you to determine the true interest level of the prospective customer. The trick to implementing this skill correctly is to make sure you are conversational in your request and that you do not try to close at this point.

## Making Futuring Conversation

When applying the futuring technique, it is best to "paint the picture" of the future event. In a casual and conversational tone, set up the scenario that is in question. If the customer says she wants to talk with a colleague, respond by saying, "So, let's say you have some free minutes a few days from now and happen to grab a cup of coffee with your colleague. The topic of my services comes up." Approaching futuring in this way gives you a subtle yet powerful way to find out what the future event may sound or look like. The concept of futuring is to transfer the customer to the future event and get her talking about it. Putting the customer in the time in question does not allow her to give you an excuse. She should be willing to answer your question directly. If there is a sign of hesitation or discomfort in the customer's answer, you are probably identifying that the customer is not as interested as she indicated and is struggling to answer your question.

## Determining the Proper Approach

The third element in dealing with futuring is to avoid the hard close. Hard-closing is counterproductive and ruins the concept of futuring. If you hard-close, you have sabotaged the underlying belief of futuring: determining your customer's true interest level. If you hard-close, it becomes all about you. If you future properly, it becomes all about the customer's answer. Therefore, it is essential to determine the proper approach to gain commitment. There are three approaches in futuring: passive, assertive, and aggressive.

### Passive Approach

The passive approach is especially useful in a newly formed relationship. It is also recommended if your prospective customer is an amiable personality type. Taking a passive approach allows you to ease into the future event. Once the picture of the future event is painted, the actual commitment statement should be, "What do you feel will happen at that time?" The passive approach is acceptable and may be the approach you want to start with. You are not demanding much from the prospective customer. You are merely asking him, to the best of his knowledge, what he feels will happen when he discusses and evaluates your product or service.

### Assertive Approach

This is my favorite approach. I like to push the envelope slightly. I like to know where I stand with respect to the existing relationship. The assertive approach steps it up a bit from the passive, yet it is dialed down from aggressive. The assertive approach asks the prospective customer if, when she talks with her peers about your product, she will recommend it over all the other choices. You've got to love this one. The magic of this approach is that you are not asking for the business; you are asking if the customer is in a position to recommend your product. Notice I just did not say simply recommend. I said, "Would you be willing to recommend my product *over all of the other choices?*" This leaves minimum room for error on your part. If you were to ask the customer whether she likes your product, if the product makes sense, if she could see the product working, and so on, you will let the customer off the hook. All these responses let the customer off the hook. You do not want that to happen. If you let her off the hook, she will swim away until next time—nibble your bait and go away again. Crafting an assertive response creates a level of accountability with respect to the customer's answer. She cannot give you a spin job. The answer should be thoughtful and complete. Anything short of a good answer suggests that the customer's interest level is not there. Practice this approach and get comfortable with it. This approach will give you the best results.

### Aggressive Approach

The third approach is aggressive—when you go for the business after all the other prior requests have failed. The aggressive approach is my least favorite, and it should be used when you have run out of things to say or when time is not on your side. The aggressive approach suggests that once you future the customer and listen to his answer to your question, you are closing hard and fast. An example of this for the customer who wants to read a study or article would be, "After you read the article and it confirms what I have been saying, will you order my product?" Some of you reading this may be thinking, "That is not so bad." Initially you are correct; it is not that bad, but being aggressive does not always permit a more consultative approach.

The aggressive approach is appropriate when the assertive approach does not work. It is also suitable if you have limited access to your customer. If you only see him a few times a year, you can use the aggressive approach to gain commitment. If you do not gain commitment, the next opportunity may be months away. And if you keep getting futured, it is quite possible a year could slip away.

By adding the futuring technique to your sales calls, you can move the customer along your closing map. If you were to receive a negative or noncommittal response to your request, you can always follow up with a reciprocal consideration choice. Introducing or reintroducing the reciprocal consideration close after the futuring response can give you a one-two, knockout punch.

# 12

# Just Because You Know Me Doesn't Mean You Are Getting More Business

Getting more business from your "friend" customer might be one of the more difficult things to do. You have a relationship, he or she is buying from you, and you are concerned that you will damage the relationship by asking for more. This chapter puts the finishing touches on how to approach the customer. It helps you realize that you might always just be "a vendor or supplier" in the customer's eyes. Few sales relationships can survive the difficulties of the economy and the ups and downs of industry if you don't give the customer more than someone else does. This chapter is to remind you to keep sharp and constantly evolve and move your relationships forward.

A few years ago, my vice president and I had a very rude awaking from one of our long-standing customers. For years, my firm provided a number of advanced training sessions for his sales team. The sessions were conducted around the country, and at the height of our relationship, we conducted over 60 programs a year. My firm was identified as a preferred provider of training services. After completing a series of training sessions on the West Coast, we were able to get a couple of minutes to unwind with our customer. During the conversation, the topic of our preferred provider status was mentioned. My vice president and I thanked him for that position and mentioned that we try to prepare, present, and deliver our programs with the utmost professionalism and passion. In passing, my VP made a comment suggesting that our long-standing relationship has enabled us not only to perform in the classroom setting, but also to get to know the customer outside of work. He went on to say how much he valued the relationship and voiced his appreciation. For the most part, it was a feel-good moment on his behalf. However, our customer's response hit us like a ton of bricks: "Remember, Jim, you are just a vendor." I shrugged the comment off as playful, but Jim did not. After the evening ended, he pulled me aside. He was upset. He asked how, after all the work that we did for the company, after the great successes it had with our content in closing multimillion-dollar deals directly related to what we had taught, how could he say that? I did not have an answer. I told him that our reward is doing an excellent job and exceeding our customer's expectations.

## Just a Vendor

Those three words took on a life of their own in our office. At the moment these words were delivered, we realized that it wasn't about the "relationship." It was about, "What can you do for me now? And can you still do it better than someone else?"

At times, salespeople get caught up in the relationship. Some customers are even viewed as friends. In the "old days" (that is relative), when my father was active in sales, I remember that he and my mother were out a couple of times a month on the weekend entertaining customers. The entertainment could range from dinners to a quick weekend away. In some cases, the relationships evolved to the point that a couple of my father's customers were invited to my wedding. That was a long, long time ago. Today, for the most part, those relationships do not happen. At best, in today's business world of rules and compliance, the most you can hope for is a strong acquaintance. During my 10-plus years as a straight-commissioned salesperson, there were only one or two customers whom I spent time with outside of work. The rest were all about business.

## All about Business

Its being all about business is a theme to keep in mind. A number of years ago, I completed a very large rollout of our content. Approximately 2,000 salespeople participated in my program. The initiative took about a year to complete. During the development and delivery of the program, my lead contact person was very cordial. He kept saying, "We need to get the families together. I enjoy working with you and your staff. I think our wives have a lot in common." Throughout the process, there was no opportunity to make this happen. When the project was finished, I reached out to the customer to see if he still wanted to get together. I did this as a courtesy and to acknowledge his prior requests. Once my project was finished and I couldn't make him look good anymore, he was not interested in the invitation. Off to the next project he went. I wasn't surprised at his response. Customers make choices they think will reflect well on themselves.

Working in a medium-to-large company requires making the right decisions. These decisions will either make or break your customers and their reputations. You will come across many different types of individuals. You may even have an interest in getting to know some customers outside of work. But remember, primarily you are the vendor or supplier he needs to make him look good.

## Familiarity Doesn't Breed More Business

Familiarity breeds contempt is an old but appropriate saying. At times we feel that our business relationships have evolved into friend relationships. When this occurs, our approach is more relaxed and less formal. In some cases that may be good; in most cases it is not recommended. Keep in mind that your top customer is your competition's top target. As soon as you slip up, the competition is waiting in the wings to take advantage. Strong business relationships can survive mistakes. Responding quickly and accurately will resolve most problems. Customers understand that situations and problems occur on occasion. The way you respond will determine their tolerance for the mistake and their willingness to continue the relationship.

## Neutralizing the Event

Problems and mistakes will occur during long-term business relationships. Managing them with the least amount of disruption to the customer will determine how well the relationship will evolve. When you receive a complaint or sense resistance from your current customer, the recommended way to manage this is to neutralize the customer using a two-part process. It is relatively easy to deflect almost any resistance and regain control of the call with just a few steps: pause, neutralize, check, and then proceed.

*Pause:* To begin neutralizing the situation, do nothing. That's right. Do nothing—this is the easy part. Pause for a second or two to consider not only what your customer's actual words were but also what they mean and how they were delivered. Pausing also serves several other purposes. When you receive an objection, complaint, or concern for the first time, you tend to think about it before you respond. You do this to regain your composure and to absorb what was just said to you. Once you process the comments, you respond. Mirroring this process will enable you to avoid the quick shoot-from-the-hip reply. Second, a strategic pause will keep your customer or prospective customer from thinking that your reply was prepackaged. It makes it seem as though you are taking his comments under consideration and are serious about the way you respond. In some cases, if you do not pause, it may appear that you are responding too quickly and not listening closely to the customer.

*Neutralize:* After pausing, neutralize what the customer has said. By neutralizing, I mean agree with the gist or concept of the customer's statement without agreeing with what he or she actually has said. For example, a number of years ago a difficult question was posed at a presidential debate. The question was focused on military spending. In response to the question, the candidate reflected for a moment and went on to explain why he was an advocate of expanding the budget to accommodate the needs of our armed forces. As I listened to the answer, I shook my head as my inner voice whispered, "You missed it. You are not connecting with your audience (in this case the American public)." I thought, if only the candidate had paused and said; "Our national security is a top priority!" Who could argue with that with everything that is happening around the world? The candidate's supporters would have cheered, and his opponents would have been left speechless. Leaving the customer speechless is not a bad thing.

If it's done properly, you temporarily eliminate the concern, because, when the customer responds to your neutralizing statement, he or she is focusing on the core issue (of the concern) and not the itemized events that caused the problem. Neutralizing can give you an opportunity to present your ideas and solutions.

*Check:* Once you believe you have identified the steps or procedures that you need to follow to resolve the concern, you should check that the customer agrees—"Does what I just presented completely resolve the issue, and can we move forward?"

*Proceed:* Then proceed to the next step. If you simply just check in with the customer, for example, "Does this make sense?" you have not clarified whether the concern has been resolved. If the customer doesn't agree that the concern has been fixed, you'll have to run through the process again.

Keep in mind that any time a customer registers concern with you, she is taking control of the call. She is moving you to the last quarter. You cannot move forward until the concern is neutralized, understood, and resolved. Once it is resolved, you go back to where you left off. As long as the two of you are still talking and you're in control of the conversation, you have a chance to alleviate the problem and advance the relationship. If the communication process starts to break down, the "business relationship" will begin to decline.

## Protecting the (Friend) Relationship

In conjunction with your ongoing contacts with your top customers and the execution of the skills that are discussed in this book, consider an additional step to protect your top customers. The concept of reciprocal consideration was introduced several chapters ago. This concept can be applied several times throughout the year to assist in the stability of your relationship with and possible growth of your top customers. The main emphasis of the technique is to apply the skill to move a prospective customer from a nonuser, to a light user, and then to a moderate user. The concept of reciprocal consideration can also be used very effectively for the friend and advocate customers. Every so often, the template of "fair to say," "reasonable," and "let's do this" can, with some modification, secure your preferred standing with your top customers and protect your relationship.

### Combining Requests for the Friend/Advocate

The advocate/friend customer can be a tricky relationship to maneuver. You want to maintain the friend atmosphere, while at the same time grow your business and market share. If this is not approached correctly, the friend/advocate may get the sense that you are in the relationship only for the money. If this occurs, the relationship can be put in jeopardy. The friend relationship can start to shut down. A discomfort and a deterioration of communication could occur. The friend/advocate has known you and your company for years. He has participated in all the educational activities, provided access, and has selected your product or service for most, if not all, of his company's applications. Essentially, this customer sees tremendous value in your product or service and is a true supporter. Your product or service is his go-to choice. Referring back to the term *schema*, this customer's mental framework selects your solution. Therefore, in this category, it is important to continue to expand the existing business as well as protect it.

To accomplish this and at the same time minimize appearing "all about the money," the application of the reciprocal consideration close can be used. The goal is to balance your desire to solidify the relationship and at the same time make sure the customer still feels it is all about the customer. To accomplish this, the following reciprocal consideration format and delivery is suggested: "Ms. Customer, is it fair to say that many of the applications you have used among our products and services are getting the results you want? Is it reasonable to believe that every so often you might receive a comment on how well things are going? Ms. Customer, please continue to use our product or service for most if not all of your applications and if, every so often, another department, company, or individual would like to hear more about our product or service, would you be willing to respond to a phone call or e-mail?"

Let's analyze this RC close. The first portion of the close is confirming that things are going well. It confirms that your product is meeting the customer's expectations. It is stating that the results are good and that there is no need to change. The second section of the RC close suggests that the customer may actually be receiving positive comments about the selection of your product or service. This section acknowledges that the customer is doing a good job, receiving recognition for his efforts, and may actually be getting rewarded for the selection of your product or service.

The "fair to say" and "reasonable" segments are targeted at the customer. If for any reason the emphasis of the close shifts to you and your product, the close will lose momentum. The third portion of the close, the "let's do this" component is asking the customer to continue and (possibly) expand the usage of your product or service. The interesting twist that occurs in this close is that it is unlike the other closes for the nonuser, light user, and/or moderate customer who were introduced in Chapter 8.

The second request of the RC close for the friend/advocate customer is designed to help you gauge the support level you have for your product or service and at the same time position the customer to provide reinforcement that your product or service is preferred. Getting the customer to respond to the request of getting him or her to speak to others is the most critical part of the close. Initially, you may think that continued use is important, and of course it is essential. Nevertheless, the second request will tell you where you are in comparison to your competition.

## Recommitting

The purpose behind the second request is not to have your existing advocate customers speak with a prospective customer to help you close more business. Certainly, when this occurs, it is a benefit. Actually, the reason behind this request is to watch how your existing customer answers the question. Will your customer willingly agree to your request? Will the customer say she would welcome the chance, but her schedule might make it difficult? Or does she dismiss the request entirely? The way the customer answers the request to talk or communicate with others will give you a true indication of the strength of your business relationship. The first two responses indicate that your relationship is on track and that the customer would be willing to help you expand your business. This means that the customer is completely satisfied and is willing to help you. It also means that if a prospective customer were to contact your existing customer by phone or e-mail, she would be willing to take the time to share all the good things that you and your product or service do. If this happens, a sales call is occurring without your being there. And most important, if a customer just told someone else how great you are, it will be difficult for the customer to have a change of heart when your competition walks through the door right after you leave! If, on the other hand, your existing customer hesitates when answering or denies your request, you know that something is wrong.

A friend/advocate of your product or service should be willing to help. If you get a negative response or a nonresponse from the friend/advocate customer, it suggests that something may not be going well. It gives you an opportunity to correct a problem before you lose the business. Test it out for yourself. Throughout the course of a year, I will contact my top customers with this request. Most times I could benefit from the reference. But occasionally I like to ask my customers the question—even if I don't need the reference—just to assess where I am in the relationship and discover where the other training vendors are positioned.

## Execution

By now I hope you recognize that you don't have to be a rocket scientist to succeed and master the concepts in this book. It is just a combination of practice, perseverance, and common sense. So here are some common sense rules to remember: No matter how long or how successfully you've been calling on a customer, the basic elements of the quarter/half/quarter model don't go away. I know I said this a few chapters ago, but this is important! And it's worth repeating.

In a maturing relationship, there is a tendency to take the easy route. After all, we've already done all the discovery research in our earlier calls. We think we know everything the customer needs. You have unquestionably established yourself as his or her partner. But because you have a maturing relationship, the risk of your story getting stale is possible. The mature relationship and the mature marketplace are reason for more homework. When your customer sees you walking down the hall or into her workspace, she needs to think, "There's Joe. (Or there's Diane.) I always have a minute or two for him or her because most times when we talk, I learn something."

## Making Sure Your Customer Never Stops Learning

The effort put forth in your pre- and postcall planning will play a considerable role in the continued success of your sales calls. Preparation is key. Let's look back to what was introduced earlier in the book. For a call to be memorable, it is important to control the pace of the call, engage the customer in dialogue, and ask a question that paints the picture of something that is happening in her job. The picture should describe a situation that will ring a bell with her. The dialogue question needs to connect with the customer. In addition, it is essential to know where you are in reference to the relationship. Where are you on the closing map? Are you halfway through the trip? You need to preselect the proper RC close that will get you to the next city. In addition to determining your RC close, prepare a backup RC close in case the call does not go well. If the call does not go well, preselect an educational RC close that you can use to keep the trip going. It is always appropriate to suggest that the customer learn more about what you are offering. In addition, anticipate the welcome that you will receive from the customer. Will it be cordial or hurried? Prepare for either situation.

## Recap

Prior to picking up the phone or getting out of your car, you need to determine the following things in order to have a successful call, regardless of whether you are calling on a friend/advocate or someone you are meeting for the first time:

1. Know how to open the call. Prepare your transition for the short or extended conversation.
2. Do your homework. Reach out to individuals to determine issues that are in need of improvement.
3. Prepare a dialogue probing question that will paint the picture of a situation, issue, or scenario that is in need of improvement to enable you to connect with the customer.
4. Know where you are on the closing map. Prepare an appropriate RC close to move the relationship forward.
5. Assume that you will get futured and craft a response.
6. Create a backup plan. If the call goes poorly, what is the alternative RC close?
7. Recap. Take the time to input call notes, customer responses, and the success of the RC close and to identify the next steps and closes.

## Don't Take Your Customers for Granted

You might say that you will never take a customer for granted. Don't bet on it. I will admit that I sometimes have taken long-time customers too much for granted myself. I've found that as my relationship with a customer deepens, I need to talk less and listen more. If you don't, you will be making a mistake, and it's important that you don't fall into that trap. Selling to an exist-

ing customer is easier than making the first sale. But do not con-
fuse easy with sure thing. There is no such thing as a sure thing.

Selling is a *discipline*. A good salesperson is disciplined. For
me, a perfect analogy here is with working out. I get up early
most mornings to exercise. It's not easy, at least for me. I may
look for excuses to turn over and go back to sleep. "I can't do it
today," I tell myself. "I worked out yesterday; I need to take a
break." Or, "It's the weekend—time to relax." You get the idea.
However, because I have a pattern and discipline about exercise
(and most things), I will roll out of bed and drag myself down-
stairs and work out.

It's important that you get up early too. It's important that
you maintain your due diligence for pre- and postcall planning.
Maintain the integrity of the quarter/half/quarter model and
your sales discipline, because it is really easy to turn over and go
back to sleep.

Clearly, you don't approach an existing customer in the same
way you approach a prospect you are meeting for the first time.
But, by the same token, you don't approach a friend in the same
way that you approach an acquaintance. Your presentation
undoubtedly will become more informal with someone you
know. Being informal is okay as long as you don't veer from the
structure of the quarter/half/quarter model.

Keep in mind that every time you introduce a new idea,
product, or service to an existing customer, the quarter/half/quar-
ter process starts all over again, just as if it were the first time. Be
cautious; just because you have a relationship with regard to your
current product or service doesn't mean that it will extend into
other areas without your doing your homework. Remember, the
competition is trying hard to get in. Practice the method that
enabled you to get in, and maintain that practice in order to keep
everyone else out.

So don't take anything for granted. However, with your existing customer, there is no need for you to introduce yourself, as you did at the beginning of your initial sales cycle. And because you've already established a common ground, you may feel that it is no longer necessary to extend the common ground by referring to articles and reports about your customer's industry. In theory, at least if you want to, now would be the time to talk about the large fish mounted behind the customer's desk.

But remember, doing your homework is what separated you from the competition in the first place. So, as informal as your sales call may become, it's still important that you have dialogue and multilayered probing questions prepared and that you have an agenda with clear and measurable objectives to gauge your progress. Your agenda must reflect your continuing desire to listen and learn.

Every relationship has its rocky periods. There are delivery schedules missed, wrong products shipped, and other commitments that go awry. Customers remember these mishaps. If you stand behind your partnership pledge, neutralize the situation, and work through the misadventures, your relationship will almost assuredly stay intact.

But chances are your customer will become a little more wary than before. Reality is never as good as a promise, under any circumstances. Remember, the trend is toward reducing the number of vendors a company uses as well as the increased propensity for customers to rely on their vendors to help find ways to meet goals and cut costs. This is another important reason that you should always keep the relationship fresh and be viewed as a resource to help the customer.

So continue to do your homework. Create meaningful discussion. Don't bore yourself or the customer. There should always be something new and interesting you can bring up to create a conversation. Be a vessel of new information. Offer new and different perspectives. Ideally, unless there has been a major blunder, you will have a good chance of introducing other products and services. After all, if you've successfully sold your customer on Product or Service A, why shouldn't he or she be open to considering selecting your Product or Service B?

## Some Final Thoughts

Don't get complacent. Continue your education. You made a choice to read this book and to continue your development. I once heard that a very famous actor was turned down by nearly 200 talent scouts. Close to 200 times, he heard the words: "No. No, we don't like you." What is interesting is that in sales, we hear, "No, we don't like your product or customer service." Rarely will you as a salesperson hear, "We don't like you!" How long could you take it if you heard no 200 times? Probably not that long. The actor realized that his rejection didn't stem from bad timing, poor roles, or typecasting. He realized that it was a reflection on his abilities. He came to understand that he couldn't control Hollywood or how hard his agent worked. He came to realize what he could control was the development of his talents and abilities. Today, this actor receives a multi-million-dollar paycheck for each film. The moral of the story is that it is not about your product, service, the economy, or whether the last person in your territory did a poor job. It is about you. It is about a commitment to going pro. It is about trying to make the all-star team. It is about getting to consecutive award trips. It does not matter if you read a hundred books or just this one, what matters is what you do with the information.

It is my hope that the information presented to you in this book will give you the tools and concepts and directions to take your sales to the next level. The material presented in this book has worked for millions of individuals—now it is your time. It is your time to restructure your questions, closes, and approaches to the customer. It is your time to have more fun. It is your time to close more sales. Enjoy the ride.

# Index

# About the Author

Charles D. Brennan, Jr., is president of Brennan Sales Institute, a Philadelphia-based consulting firm that has been providing advanced sales training programs for more than 25 years. He is also the author of the bestselling *Sales Questions That Close the Sale* (1994) and the award-winning *Proactive Customer Service* (1997).